THE GREEK LANGUAGE

THE GREEK LANGUAGE

BY

GEORGE THOMSON

Professor of Greek in the University of Birmingham
and formerly Fellow of King's College Cambridge;
Member of the Czechoslovak Academy of Sciences

Καί μέσ' στῆς χρυσοπράσινης νυχτιᾶς τὰ βάθη
'Ακόμ' ἀργολαλεῖ τοῦ Κολωνοῦ τἀηδόνι.

PALAMAS

CAMBRIDGE
W. HEFFER & SONS LTD
1966

First published 1960
Reprinted with corrections and additions 1966

PRINTED BY E. J. BRILL, THE NETHERLANDS

To the memory of

NICHOLAS BACHTIN

CONTENTS

CONTENTS

IX

PREFACE TO THE FIRST EDITION

During the past fifty years classical studies have lost the commanding position they once held in our educational system. They have had to make room for newer subjects, such as modern languages and the natural sciences. That is as it should be. But they have not been reorganised in conformity with the new conditions. The methods of teaching have remained substantially unchanged, and the result is that the decline has been greater than it need have been. At most universities it is still assumed that students offering classics will have devoted several years to Greek and Latin at school.

The method of teaching Greek established at Birmingham University has been worked out gradually over the past twenty years. Its principal features can be best explained by contrasting it with the system it replaced.

Under the old system, the course for the degree of B.A. was designed for students of the ordinary kind, who had studied the two languages up to the required standard at school. Provision was made, however, for those who had no previous knowledge of Greek. They spent a preliminary year doing Elementary Greek, another year taking the Intermediate Course, and then entered the School of Classics, making five years in all. In special cases they might be admitted to the School of Classics after completing the Elementary Course. It was clear, however, that these students were severely handicapped. Accordingly, it was decided to reconstruct the Greek part of the degree course so as to make it equally suitable for both types of student and at the same time to reconstruct the Elementary Course so that it might be thrown open to other students as a subsidiary subject.

The immediate obstacle to any reform of this kind was the regular practice of unprepared translation and prose composition, which accordingly was abolished. The weakness of unprepared translation, from an educational point of view, is that the problems it poses are artificial problems. Translation from Greek into English, if pursued on the basis of a comparative study of the two languages, raises many linguistic problems, which being real provide a far more satisfying and effective intellectual training. As for composition, it rests on the mistaken assumption that it is possible to write correctly a language of which the writer has at best a very imperfect knowledge and which he cannot speak. This limitation applies even to mature scholars, though many of them are unaware of it. The so-called 'fair copies' are spurious. The errors they contain only escape notice because their authors adopt a subjective, unscientific—even anti-scientific—attitude to the language, which is transmitted to the students.

By abolishing composition a further obstacle was removed. The beginner who will be required to write Attic prose must begin with Attic Greek. When that requirement is dropped, he is free to begin with Homeric Greek, which gives him a better start from every point of view. The Homeric poems are the earliest works of Greek literature we possess. Starting with them, we start at the beginning. Experience has shown that it is easier to proceed from Homeric Greek to Attic than to proceed in the reverse direction. This is true both of the language and of the literature. There is nothing in Attic literature that can be enjoyed with so little previous explanation as the Iliad or Odyssey. Thus, by starting with Homer, the learner's task is made both lighter and more methodical; for he is studying both the language and the literature in the order of their historical development.

Accordingly, in our Elementary Course we begin with Homeric Greek. The course lasts for one session and consists of three hours' teaching a week. At the end of it the students have acquired the rudiments of the language and read two books of the Odyssey. Having completed the course, those who are taking Greek as a subsidiary subject will give it up; but even they have gone far enough to continue it on their own, if they wish, and some of them do. The others enter the School of Classics, where they join forces with students from school who have done Greek for several years. How are the two streams merged? To answer this question a little more must be said about the content of the Elementary Course.

When we began work on this course, we approached the problem from a purely empirical point of view: that is to say, our aim was to make Greek easier to learn, so that it could be learnt more quickly. But we soon discovered that the quickest way to learn Greek is to study it scientifically. Accordingly, we set about replacing descriptive grammar with historical linguistics. The method of descriptive grammar is to teach the language by means of rules and exceptions, which the student learns by rote without understanding how the rules came into being or why they should be subject to exceptions. This method is slow and wasteful. The method of historical linguistics is to teach the language from the standpoint of its origin and development as an organic unity. Taught in this way, it is not only easier to learn, but the process of learning it, instead of being merely a means to an end, becomes also an end in itself; it acquires an intrinsic value as a training in scientific method, which the student can, and does, apply to other languages, including his own. In this way he is led to perceive that behind the study of a particular language lies the study of language as such—the science of linguistics—which is linked up on every side with other subjects, such as literature, history, psychology and philosophy.

The students who enter the School of Classics from the Elementary Course find that, in comparison with the other students, their reading is very limited; but they have learnt the language from a different point of view, which to the others is entirely new. This serves to redress the balance. The work of the first year includes a course on comparative Indo-European philology, with special reference to Ancient Greek, followed in the second year by a course on the history of the Greek language from the earliest times down to the present day. This training in historical linguistics provides both an intellectual discipline and a knowledge of the language superior to any that can be obtained from composition and unprepared translation.

Our procedure in the Elementary Course is as follows. It opens with an introductory section, lasting about six weeks. The distribution of the language at successive periods is shown on a map. After explaining the principles of linguistics we pass to the origins of writing and the alphabet (Tables I-III). Care is taken to present only the minimum of factual material and at the same time to warn the students that such a procedure necessarily involves over-simplification and that some of the data are conjectural. After a general discussion of inflection, word-order and accentuation, we examine in detail the morphology of the noun and verb (Tables VI-XI). The categories of case, number, gender, voice, mood, tense and aspect are studied historically, and the personal endings of the verb (excluding the dual) are reduced phonologically to a basic set of six. This completes the introductory section. The students have already begun the Odyssey, and the rest of the course is devoted to reading, the further work on morphology and syntax being treated incidentally in connection with the text. The introductory section is designed to arouse the student's interest in the science of linguistics and on this basis to construct a theoretical framework within which the actual forms of the language can be built up systematically and so committed to memory with the minimum of conscious effort. In the ensuing part of the course, the student tends to forget, not the forms themselves, which are kept before him in his reading, but the theoretical framework in which he has learnt them. This does not matter, because it has served its immediate purpose, and, if he continues the subject, he has an opportunity of reconstructing it on a broader basis in the following year.

These reforms have been effected without reducing the students' reading. On the contrary, it has been increased. Those who graduate now have read more than four times as much literature, at least three times as much philosophy, and twice as much history as those who graduated under the old system. At the same time, composition, in the form of re-translation (which ensures that the 'fair copies' are really fair), is available as an optional subject for those who wish to take it up or continue it; and, thanks to their wide reading, they are in the best possible position to do so.

And yet, it may be urged, there is surely one virtue in composition for which no substitute can be found in this or any other method. Composition is creative. It may be granted that composition has some value as a creative exercise for those who enjoy it (for the rest it is deadly); and therefore, if composition is to be abandoned, some other form of creative activity—if possible, a better one—should be provided. What should it be?

It is strange that so many classical scholars visiting Greece to refresh themselves at the fount of Hellenism should spend all their time contemplating the material remains of antiquity without realising that the object of their quest still flows from the lips of the people. The relation between Ancient and Modern (spoken) Greek is so close that they are treated by all authorities, not as two languages, like Latin and Italian, but as one. The difference between Modern Greek and Homer is estimated to be no greater than the difference between Modern English and *Piers Plowman*, though there is a span of twenty-eight centuries in the one case and only six in the other. Hence, an English student reading Euripides with no knowledge of Modern Greek is at the same disadvantage as a foreign student reading Chaucer with no knowledge of Modern English. No foreign student of English would be so misguided as to cut himself off from the living source, and the student who approaches Greek in this way develops a creative activity which is real, not artificial, and finds that the ancient language springs to life.

Accordingly, in their second and third years, our students take a course in Modern Greek, devoted to conversation, essay-writing and reading (ballads, lyrics, short stories). In this way they are introduced to the riches of medieval and modern Greek literature. They have the opportunity of following the history of the Greek people—its language, literature and civilisation—over a period of nearly three thousand years. There is no other language, with the single exception of Chinese, that offers so long a historical perspective.

This little book contains the material used for the three courses I have mentioned—the Elementary Course, the course on Indo-European philology, and the course on the history of the language,—except that for the second we also use T. Hudson-Williams' *Short Introduction to the Study of Comparative Grammar (Indo-European)*. The material has been rearranged in a form suitable for continuous reading. Chapter I, dealing with grammatical categories, has been included for the sake of all those students, who, owing to the deplorably low level of English language teaching in this country, leave school with little or no theoretical understanding of their own language. The remainder falls into four parts: a presentation of the general principles of linguistics (Chapters II-III); an account of Ancient Greek, followed by a history of the language as a whole (Chapters IV-XIV); a selection of illustrative texts; and a set of grammatical tables. The Linear B texts are not dealt with, because the results so far obtained from the Ventris-Chadwick decipherment are, in my opinion, inconclusive. All the material has been presented as concisely as possible in order that the book might be available at a price that students can afford.

It is dedicated to the late Nicholas Bachtin, a pupil of Meillet and Psicharis, and one of the most brilliant intellects I have known. He was by nature a poet, but, compelled by circumstances to forgo the writing of poetry, he devoted himself to the science of language, to which he brought, besides wide knowledge and exact scholarship, a poet's passion. He taught me to place my knowledge of the language on a scientific basis. With him I learnt Greek all over again. The inspiration of this book is his.

I am also indebted to my colleague and former pupil, Mr. R. F. Willetts, who has taken over the Elementary Course and introduced many improvements; and we are both indebted to our students. The problems involved in working out a new approach to the teaching of the language have been discussed with them year by year and could not have been solved without their co-operation.

Finally, I wish to express my warmest thanks to Mr. John Chadwick, who has read the book in MS and made a large number of criticisms and corrections. He is not responsible for any errors that remain.

Birmingham, 1959   GEORGE THOMSON

PREFACE TO THE SECOND EDITION

The reception accorded to this book encourages me to think that it has helped to meet a real need among those who are interested in re-forming the traditional method of teaching Greek.

Since the first edition was prepared, we have organised, in addition to our beginners' course in Homeric Greek, a parallel course in Attic, based on Plato's *Crito*. It is intended mainly for students of theology, for whom it has the advantage that, besides giving them a historical approach to the language of the New Testament, it prepares them for the Atticistic Greek of the Christian Fathers.

This experiment has been completely successful, but it has confirmed me in the opinion that, for students of Classical Greek, Homer makes a better beginning. The view, which is still widely held among professional scholars, that Homeric Greek is more difficult for beginners than Attic, is unfounded.

For those who read Modern Greek, a short history of the language, based on the present work, is now available in my book Ἡ ἑλληνικὴ γλῶσσα ἀρχαία καὶ νέα (Athens, 1964). I have also completed a primer of Modern Greek, which is due to be published shortly.

This edition includes a number of corrections and additions.

Birmingham, 1965   GEORGE THOMSON

I. GRAMMATICAL CATEGORIES

1. *The sentence.* Speech is composed of sentences. A sentence is a group of words expressing a relationship between two or more concepts in a form which is structurally complete, that is, fully articulate: (1) 'God is'; (2) 'God is good'; (3) 'God wills'. The concept 'God' is related in the first sentence to the concept of existence, in the second to the concept of goodness, in the third to the concept of willing. On the other hand, the expressions 'God's goodness', 'God's will', 'God willing' are not sentences, because they are not structurally complete. The sentence is the organic unit of speech.

2. *The word.* The words composing a sentence may be divided into two kinds: those which express concepts ('full words' or semantemes) and those which express relationships between concepts ('empty words' or morphemes). The distinction is not absolute. Thus, in the sentence 'God is good', the words 'God' and 'good' are full words, expressing concepts, whereas 'is' is an empty word, expressing merely a certain relationship between them; but in the sentence 'God is' the word 'is' is a full word, expressing both the concept of existence and its relation to the concept 'God'. An empty word may be only part of a word as commonly understood. Thus, we say 'I am the father of John' and 'I am John's father'. Here the full words are 'father' and 'John', whereas both 'of' and '-s' are empty words, expressing the relationship between the full words.

3. *Inflections.* An empty word of the type '-s' in 'John's' is called an inflection. The word 'drink' has the inflections 'drinks', 'drank', 'drunk', 'drunken' etc.

4. *The noun.* Full words may be divided into two main classes: nouns and verbs. A noun expresses a concept regarded as an entity or quality ('God', 'good'); a verb expresses a concept regarded as an action or process ('drinks', 'is'). The noun may be a proper noun ('God', 'John') or a common noun ('father'). It may also be a substantive ('God', 'John', 'father') or an adjective ('good'). A substantive is the name of an entity; an adjective is the name of a quality as it appertains to a substantive. Adjectives are used to qualify substantives in two ways: attributively, that is, by attaching the adjective directly to the substantive, so that the

two form a single substantival phrase ('a good king'); or predicatively, that is, by combining the two through the medium of a verb so as to form a sentence ('The king is good'). The pronoun, as its name implies, is a word used in place of a noun. It may be used as a substantive ('He is a good king') or as an adjective ('This king is good').

5. *Declension.* The declension of a noun is the series of modifications to which it is subjected by the process of inflection. In English, the adjective has no inflections except those which mark differences of degree: 'happy' (positive), 'happier' (comparative), 'happiest' (superlative). The substantive is inflected according to number (singular and plural): 'king' 'kings', 'goose' 'geese'. In Old English, as in Greek and Latin, the noun had two sets of inflections, called *cases*, one for the singular and one for the plural, designed to mark different grammatical relations. The ending '-s' in 'John's father' is properly a case ending.

6. *The verb.* The verb has different forms to distinguish the agent, time and quality of the action or process which it denotes. The forms distinguishing the agent are called *persons*. The English verb has six persons: first ('I drink'), second ('You drink') and third ('He *or* she *or* it drinks') persons singular; first ('We drink'), second ('You drink') and third ('They drink') persons plural. The forms marking the time are called *tenses*: 'I drink' or 'I am drinking' (present), 'I drank' or 'I was drinking' (past), 'I shall drink' (future). The forms marking the quality are of two kinds, *aspects* and *moods*. There are two aspects, perfective and imperfective. The perfective aspect marks the action as complete ('I drink', 'I drank', 'I shall drink'); the imperfective marks it as incomplete ('I am drinking', 'I was drinking', 'I shall be drinking'). In English there are four moods: indicative ('I drink', I drank' etc.), subjunctive ('I may drink'), conditional ('I should drink'), imperative ('Drink!'). All these forms of the verb are *finite*, that is, they are sufficient in themselves to constitute a sentence. Regarding them as a series, we speak of the *conjugation* of the verb, corresponding to the declension of the noun.

7. *Voice.* There are also different forms of the verb indicating whether the action which it denotes is regarded as active or passive. Thus, when we say 'All men eat bread', the verb is in the active voice, marking 'all men' as the agents; but when we say 'Bread is eaten', it is in the passive voice, indicating that bread is not the agent but that which is acted on.

8. *Verbal nouns.* In addition to the finite forms of the verb, there are verbal substantives and verbal adjectives, which differ from ordinary

substantives and adjectives in that they exist in different forms according to tense and voice. There are two kinds of verbal substantive, (1) the *infinitive*, and (2) the *gerund*: (1) 'to drink' (active), 'to be drunk' (passive), 'to drink' (present), 'to have drunk' (past), 'to be drinking' (present imperfective) etc.; (2) 'drinking' (active present), 'having drunk' (active past) etc. Examples: 'To drink is dangerous', 'Drinking is dangerous', 'Seeing is believing'. The verbal adjective is called a *participle*: 'drinking' (active), 'drunk' (passive) etc. Examples: 'I watched the drinking horses' (attributive), 'I watched the horses drinking' (predicative), 'I saw the wine drunk', etc.

9. *Auxiliary verbs.* Several of the verbal forms given above consist of an infinitive or participle constructed with the verb 'to be' or other verbs such as 'may' 'shall' 'will' 'should' etc. These are called auxiliary verbs, that is, are used as empty words.

10. *Subject and predicate.* Every sentence may be divided into subject and predicate. The subject is a noun; the predicate contains a finite verb. The subject is that of which the rest of the sentence tells us (predicates) something ('*The water* is boiling'); the predicate is what we are told of the subject ('The water *is boiling*'). The distinction between subject and predicate applies even where the sentence consists of only one word, e.g. 'Drink!' (imperative). Here the verb, being in the second person, conveys the idea of an agent (the subject) as well as an action (the predicate).

11. *Nominal and verbal sentences.* Having regard to the subject and predicate, we may distinguish between two types of sentence, nominal and verbal. In the nominal sentence, the predicate is a noun connected with the subject by the empty word 'is', which in this usage is called the *copula*: 'God is good'. In the verbal sentence, the idea which is predicated of the subject is expressed wholly or partly in a verb: 'God is', 'All men eat bread'. The verb in the verbal sentence may be *intransitive* or *transitive*. If intransitive, it denotes an action regarded as complete in itself ('All men eat'); if transitive, it is constructed with a noun denoting the *object* to which the action of the verb is directed ('All men eat bread'). Subject and object are normally distinguished by their position in relation to the verb: 'Sheep eat grass'. A transitive verb may have two objects, direct and indirect: 'He gave me the book', where 'the book' is the direct object and 'me' is the indirect object.

12. *Adverbs and prepositions.* Just as the substantive is qualified by an adjective, so the verb is qualified by an adverb: 'a just king', 'He rules justly'. The adverb is also used to qualify adjectives: 'He is justly

famous'. Many words, originally adverbs, have become attached to nouns and verbs as *prepositions*: 'He fell over' (adverb), 'He fell over the stool' (preposition), 'to overlook'. Most prepositions may be used either concretely or abstractly, the former usage being the older: 'over the wall', 'over a shilling'.

13. *Statements, questions and commands.*   Except where the verb is in the imperative, every sentence consists either of a statement, affirmative or negative, or of a question: 'The water is warm', 'The water is not warm', 'Is the water warm?' 'Is not the water warm?'. When used in questions, the negative particle ('not') imparts to the question an expectation that the answer will be affirmative: 'Is not the water warm? Yes, it is'. Questions are also introduced by interrogative pronouns and adverbs: 'Who is there?', 'Where are you?'. Where the verb is in the imperative, the sentence is either a command (affirmative) or a prohibition (negative).

14. *Compound sentences.*   The simple sentence contains, in its simplest form, only one finite verb. If there is more than one, they are co-ordinated with one another, usually by means of a connecting particle such as 'and' or 'but': 'Men eat and drink', 'The horse is eating but he will not drink'. The compound sentence contains, besides the *principal clause*, one or more *subordinate clauses*, which stand to the principal clause in the relation of substantive, adjective or adverb. Thus, we may speak of substantival, adjectival and adverbial clauses.

15. *Substantival clauses* fall into two main classes: (1) subject clauses, and (2) object clauses: (1) 'That you were once unkind befriends me now'; (2) 'I never saw that you did painting need'. The particle (or conjunction) 'that' (in origin a pronoun) introduces the subordinate clause, which serves in the first instance as the subject of the principal verb and in the second as the object. Sometimes the particle is omitted: 'My glass shall not persuade me I am old'. The subject clause may be deferred, its place before the verb being taken by the pronoun 'it': ' 'Tis not enough that through the cloud thou break'.

16. *Adjectival clauses*, commonly known as relative clauses, are introduced by a relative pronoun referring to a noun in the principal clause, which is called its *antecedent*: 'This thou perceiv'st, which makes thy love more strong, To love that well which thou must leave ere long'.

17. *Adverbial clauses* qualify the verb of the principal clause or the principal clause as a whole. They may be classified as follows: (1) *final*, expressing purpose, introduced by the particles 'that' or 'in order that' (negative 'lest'); (2) *consecutive*, expressing a consequence or result

('so that'); (3) *concessive*, expressing a limitation or reservation ('though');
(4) *causal*, expressing a cause or reason ('because', 'since'); (5) *modal*,
expressing the manner or a comparison ('as', 'just as'); (6) *temporal*,
expressing the time ('when', 'since', 'after'); (7) *local*, expressing the place
('where'); (8) *conditional*, expressing a condition or hypothesis ('if',
'unless'). Examples: (1) 'From fairest creatures we desire increase That
thereby beauty's rose might never die'; (2) 'For thy sweet love remembered such wealth brings That then I scorn to change my state with
kings'; (3) 'Though thou repent, yet have I still the loss'; (4) 'Since
there's no help, come let us kiss and part'; (5) 'Like as the waves make
towards the pebbled shore, So do our minutes hasten to their end'; (6)
'When most I wink, then do mine eyes best see; For all the day they
view things unrespected, But, when I sleep, in dreams they look on thee';
(7) 'Thou art the grave where buried love doth live'; (8) 'For, if I should
despair, I should grow mad'.

18. *Conditional sentences* may be classified as follows: (1) open, giving
no indication regarding the fulfilment of the condition; (2) half-open,
implying that the fulfilment of the condition is somewhat remote; and
(3) closed, indicating that the condition is unrealised or unrealisable. Open
conditions may be present, past or future; half-open conditions are future;
closed conditions are present or past. Examples: (1) 'If it is raining, the
grass is wet' (open present); 'If it was raining, the grass was wet' (open
past); 'If it rains, the grass will be wet' (open future); (2) 'If it were to
rain, the grass would be wet' (half-open); (3) 'If it were raining, the grass
would be wet' (closed present); 'If it had been raining, the grass would
have been wet' (closed past).

II. LINGUISTICS

1. *Linguistics.* The science of linguistics has three main branches:
general linguistics, dealing with the origin and nature of speech; comparative linguistics, dealing with the relations between languages; and
historical linguistics, dealing with the evolution of languages as determined
by social and historical conditions. The subject-matter of linguistics falls
into three parts: phonetics, dealing generally with the sounds used in
speech, and also with the sounds used in particular languages (phonology);
grammar, dealing with the formation of words (morphology) and sentences (syntax); and lexicology, dealing with words as expressions of

ideas and with their derivation (etymology) and changes of meaning (semantics).

2. *General linguistics.* Speech was evolved as a means of communication by men engaged in social production. The faculty of speech and the use of tools are distinctively human characteristics. As he invented tools and speech, man became capable of thinking, that is, of forming general concepts. Speech enabled the members of the community to share their experiences with one another and to transmit them collectively from generation to generation. Human evolution ceased to be a purely biological process, like that of the animals, and became social. A fuller understanding of the origin of speech may be expected when the linguistic data have been studied in the light of recent physiological research on the functioning of the brain. Since speech and thought are functions of society, the origin of grammatical and logical categories is to be sought in social activity. Little work has yet been done in this field. Since language changes more slowly than society, the evidence of language may be used to throw light on the past. If many linguistic phenomena are still unexplained, it is largely because we lack the requisite historical knowledge. Whereas man is about a million years old, the earliest written documents are less than six thousand years old, and the great majority of languages are known to us over only a fraction of that period. During that time they have been in continuous contact with one another, influencing one another and replacing one another. It is well known that a people may abandon its own language and adopt the language of another people: for example, the Normans, the Irish, and the American negroes. There is no necessary connection between language and race.

3. *Comparative linguistics.* By comparing different languages it is possible to classify them according to their mutual affinities. The languages of the world are divided into a number of families. The family to which our own language belongs is called Indo-European (IE). It may be related distantly to the Finno-Ugrian family (Finnish and Hungarian) and still more distantly to the Semitic (Hebrew, Arabic). The principal IE languages are set out in Table I. It will be seen that they are arranged on the assumption that they are all descended from a single parent language, called Common Indo-European. Common Indo-European stands to the IE languages in the same relation as Latin to the Romance languages (Italian, French, Spanish, Portuguese, Rumanian). If Latin had perished, it could still have been reconstructed to some extent by a comparative analysis of the languages descended from it (Table II B). Common Indo-European has been reconstructed in the same way (Table II A).

It must be remembered, however, that, whereas Latin is known to us from written records, Common Indo-European is a purely hypothetical construct.

4. *Historical linguistics.*   The aim of historical linguistics is to study a language in the process of growth through successive stages of development, as opposed to descriptive linguistics, in which the language is studied as it exists at a given stage of its development. Descriptive linguistics is useful and necessary for certain purposes, but it is subject to this limitation, that, if we study a language at a given stage of development, without reference to the preceding stages, we are unable to explain many of its features or even to describe them correctly. For example, the deponent verb in Latin is commonly described as being passive in form and active in meaning; but, when we examine it historically, we find that it is really, in form and meaning, a survival of the old middle voice. All languages are always changing, and therefore every language contains at every stage of its development anomalies which can only be understood in the light of its previous development.

5. *The Greek language.*   Modern Greek is spoken in Greece, Crete, Cyprus, a few villages in southern Italy and Sicily, and in Istanbul, Alexandria and many other cities throughout the world. Before the second world war it was spoken in parts of the Crimea and Transcaucasia and before 1922 in the west and north of Anatolia. Ancient Greek was spoken in Greece, Crete, Cyprus and other parts of the eastern Mediterranean, in western and northern Anatolia, on the north coast of the Black Sea, in southern Italy and eastern Sicily, and at some points on the African coast and the French Riviera. The earliest documents written in the Greek alphabet date from the eighth century B.C., but it is probable that the language had been spoken in eastern and southern Greece at least as far back as 1500 B.C.

6. *The history of Greek.*   Of all the European languages Greek has the longest and fullest recorded history. Its evolution can be followed continuously from the seventh century B.C. down to the present day. Latin is known only from the third century B.C., and Low Latin, parent of the Romance languages, is very poorly documented in comparison with Greek. The Celtic, Germanic and Slavonic languages are known only from the VI-IXth centuries A.D. Further, Ancient Greek is known to us in a number of dialects, providing material for comparative analysis, which enables us to reconstruct in outline its prehistoric form. For the present purpose we shall distinguish the following stages in the evolution of the language: (1) Prehistoric Greek (PG); (2) Ancient Greek (AG), divided

into Classical Greek (CG), down to the death of Alexander the Great (323 B.C.), and Hellenistic Greek (HG), down to the foundation of Constantinople (330 A.D.); (3) Byzantine Greek (BG), down to the sack of Constantinople in the Fourth Crusade (1204 A.D.); and (4) Modern Greek (MG). BG and MG overlap to a marked degree. On the one hand, the literary language of BG, based on AG, has persisted in a modified form to this day; on the other hand, in the spoken language, many of the characteristics of MG can be traced back to the Hellenistic period, and they were well established by the eleventh century A.D. One of the characteristics of the language, due to the fact that it has been highly cultivated from early in the first millennium B.C. down to the present day, is the strength and continuity of the literary tradition, favouring the survival of old forms alongside the new.

III. LINGUISTIC CHANGE

1. *Lexical changes.* The introduction of a new word, whether to express a new idea or to replace an old word that has lost its force, is a more or less conscious process. The new word may be formed from indigenous elements, or it may be borrowed from another language. The vocabulary of some languages, such as English and Greek, is largely of foreign origin. The words that last longest are those which express simple or homely ideas, because, as the first to be learnt by the child, they are the most deeply imprinted on its memory, e.g. the terms of relationship, numerals, and words expressing such ideas as eating, drinking, sleeping, coming, going etc. Such words form what is called the basic word stock, which changes more slowly than the rest of the vocabulary. In general, words change less rapidly than their meanings, and hence their etymology may be historically significant: μοῖρα (1) share, (2) lot, (3) fate; κλῆρος (1) lot, (2) holding of land, (3) inheritance, (4) clergy; δουλεία (AG) slavery, (HG) service, (MG) work.

2. *Grammatical changes* take place for the most part unconsciously. The grammar of a language is more lasting than its vocabulary. Grammatical changes are not regular: they occur in some words but not in others, and so give rise to anomalies, which are only resolved by further changes. The words most resistant to morphological change are those belonging to the basic word stock: thus, in all the IE languages the verb 'to be' is irregular, that is, archaic. The evolution of the IE languages shows a general but uneven tendency towards morphological simplification.

3. *Phonetic changes*, or sound changes, are unconscious and regular.

We may speak, therefore, of phonetic laws; but these differ from natural laws, because they vary, not only in different languages, but in different periods of the same language. The total number of simple sounds (phonemes) that can be produced by the vocal organs is virtually infinite, but few languages possess more than fifty. The phonemes used in a given language constitute its phonetic system. (For the AG phonetic system see Table IV). This system is an organic unity, in which even a small change produces others, with the result that it is eventually transformed; yet, though subject to radical changes over long periods, it is, as used by individual speakers, almost fixed. Having been acquired in early childhood by unconscious adaptation of the vocal organs, it resists even conscious efforts to change it. We all know how foreigners speak English with a foreign accent, that is, with the phonemes of their own language. Similarly, when a people changes its language, like the Welsh and Irish, the phonetic system of the old language is carried over into the new. Neighbouring peoples tend to become bilingual and so to develop common features in their phonetic systems. Such changes, called external changes, must have operated continuously at all times, because no people has ever lived in isolation. In order to explain them all, we should need to know all the languages involved, which is impossible. There are also internal changes, whose nature, in so far as they can be distinguished from external changes, is still obscure. Learning to speak is a long process; no two individuals speak exactly alike; no language remains the same from one generation to the next. As children grow up, the grosser deviations are eliminated; but others, too minute to be perceptible, persist and spread. In primitive communities, which are small in numbers and in which personal prestige counts for much, even individual idiosyncrasies may have lasting effects. It seems that languages change most rapidly at times when intensive external contacts combine with an accumulation of internal changes to produce a condition of relative instability, as in HG.

4. *Consecutive changes.* Phonetic changes may lead to grammatical changes and these in turn to lexical changes. Thus, PG had a single set of inflections for the imperfect and aorist, which may be illustrated as follows. First person singular: imperfect *ἔγραφον, aorist (thematic) *ἔμνθον, (sigmatic) *ἔγραψν. Third person plural: imperfect *ἔγραφοντ, aorist (thematic) *ἔμνθοντ, (sigmatic) *ἔγραψντ. Here we have two inflections, one for each person. In AG, owing to the transformation of -ν into -α after a consonant, the first person singular became ἔγραφον ἔμαθον ἔγραψα; and, owing to the loss of final -τ, the third person plural became ἔγραφον ἔμαθον ἔγραψαν (-αν with -α- borrowed

from the first person singular). Here we have two persons with one inflection (1 sg. 3 pl. ἔγραφον ἔμαθον) and two inflections for one person (1 sg. ἔμαθον ἔγραψα). This situation was anomalous and unstable. In the Ionic dialect the quasi-sigmatic aorist εἶπα εἶπαν for εἶπον εἶπον is as old as Homer, and in HG this type was developed: ἔμαθα ἔμαθαν for ἔμαθον ἔμαθον. In MG the two tenses have been reconstructed as follows: ἔγραφα ἔγραφαν, ἔμαθα ἔμαθαν, ἔγραψα ἔγραψαν. In this way the prehistoric equilibrium has been restored. See further XIII.3.7.

5. *Analogy*. Analogical changes are changes due to the association of different forms or different words in the speaker's mind. They affect the language in all its aspects—morphological, lexical, syntactical. Thus, the quasi-sigmatic aorist εἶπα was formed by analogy from the true sigmatic aorist ἔλυσα. Similarly, in the sigmatic aorist itself the third plural ending ἔλυ-σαν was extended by analogy to the aorist indicative passive ἐλύθησαν (Ep. ἔλυθεν from *ἐλυθεντ) and later to the imperative (λυέτω λυέτωσαν on the analogy of ἐλύθη ἐλύθησαν). Further examples of morphological analogy will be found in the evolution of the verb 'to be': see Table XIII. Examples of lexical analogy are ἐμποδών after ἐκποδών, μηκέτι after οὐκέτι, ἀνδράποδα after τετράποδα. Syntactical analogy may be illustrated by the so-called accusative-and-infinitive construction: (1) ἀδικεῖν σέ φημι 'I say you are guilty', lit. 'I declare you to be guilty', σε being the direct object of φημί, while the infinitive (properly the dative of a verbal noun) is a complement; (2) πέπεισμαί σε ἀδικεῖν 'I am convinced that you are guilty': here σε must be construed with ἀδικεῖν as an object clause.

6. *Dialect and writing*. Among preliterate peoples there exist marked differences of speech between adjacent districts and even adjacent villages, and there is no obstacle to their development beyond the needs of mutual intercourse. The aggregate of such local varieties in a given region constitutes a dialect. Dialect divisions are not definite but are nevertheless sufficiently clear to give the people the consciousness of speaking a distinctive form of the common language. There is no difference in principle between a group of dialects and a family of languages. The question whether a given vernacular is a dialect or a language can only be determined in the light of the social and historical conditions. Some of the AG dialects differed so widely that they can hardly have been mutually intelligible; yet their speakers were all conscious of possessing a common language. With the growth of trade, the introduction of writing, and the rise of the state, the relation between the dialects is transformed by the emergence of a literary or standard dialect. Generally,

the dialect of the region in which the state is centred asserts itself, with modifications derived from other dialects, as the standard form of the language, officially recognised as the written medium of commerce and government, cultivated by the ruling class and gradually extending its influence into the provincial regions until the old dialects sink to the level of patois. The standard form of the language is by its nature resistant to change and so tends to retard, though it can never arrest, the evolution of the language. If it falls behind the spoken language so far as to become unintelligible to the common people, it is doomed sooner or later to extinction, because it has ceased to fulfil the primary function of language, which is to serve as a means of communication for society as a whole.

7. *Grammatical categories.*   Not only are the concrete phenomena of language subject to change, but so too are the grammatical categories which we use to classify them. The categories with which we are familiar were formulated originally to describe the structure of Ancient Greek (which served also as the basis of Aristotelian logic) and adapted subsequently to Latin. The middle voice and the optative mood disappeared from Latin: that is to say, the modifications in the meaning of the verb which the AG middle and optative had served to indicate were expressed in other ways without the use of these formal categories. Again, the categories of voice, mood, gender, case (which do not exist at all in many non-IE languages), have become merely nominal in some IE languages, such as English, being retained out of deference to tradition. Thus, we say that in English, as in Latin, the verb has two voices, active and passive: 'I wash', 'I am washed'. If we admit 'I am washed' as a passive, there is no reason, apart from convention, why we should not also admit 'I wash (for) myself' as a middle (VIII.1) ; and in fact, as a formal category, the passive does not exist in English except in the participle 'washed'. Bearing in mind the element of relativity in grammatical (and hence also in logical) categories, the student of language will treat with reserve the work of philosophers who investigate language without any knowledge of linguistics, just as the physiologist treats with reserve the psychologists who investigate consciousness without any training in physiology.

IV. THE ALPHABET

1. *Modern alphabets.*   An alphabet is a script in which each sign represents in principle a single consonant or vowel. All the alphabets in

use to-day are of common origin. The Roman and the Russian are derived from the Greek; the Greek from the Phoenician; the Hebrew and the Arabic from the Aramaic. The Phoenician and the Aramaic, which are closely related, were evolved in Palestine early in the second millennium B.C. They are derived partly from Egyptian hieroglyphics and partly from Babylonian cuneiform. These Egyptian and Babylonian scripts were pre-alphabetic.

2. *Pre-alphabetic scripts.*   Three stages may be distinguished in the evolution of writing prior to the invention of the alphabet: (1) pictographic, (2) ideographic, (3) phonographic. In the first stage the unit is the pictogram, which is simply a picture of the object it denotes: for example, an eye is represented by a picture of an eye. In the second stage the unit is the ideogram, derived in most cases from the pictogram but simplified in form and extended in meaning. Thus, water is represented by a wavy line, and the signs for eye and water are combined to mean 'weep'. In the third stage the unit is the phonogram, which denotes a particular sound or group of sounds. Thus, the Egyptian sign for ro 'mouth' was originally a picture of an open human mouth (pictogram); this was then reduced to a simple oval (ideogram); and later it came to be used for the sound ro wherever it occurred, without regard to its meaning (phonogram).

3. *The Phoenician alphabet.*   The Babylonian cuneiform script (so called from the fact that every sign is made up of wedge-shaped strokes) was systematised as a syllabary: that is, each sign denoted a particular combination of consonant and vowel. The Egyptian script was never systematised. It remained a jumble of pictograms, ideograms and phonograms, and even included a few alphabetical signs. Thus, the sign ro came to be used for the consonant r. It was left to the Semites, and particularly the Phoenicians, to develop this principle. The Phoenicians reorganised the Egyptian signs as an alphabet of 22 characters. There were no vowel signs. One of the morphological characteristics of the Semitic family of languages is its extensive use of vowel gradation (cf. sing sang sung song), which made it easy for the reader to supply the vowels from the context. The Phoenician signs are related to the Egyptian in form and meaning but not in their phonetic value. Thus, the Phoenician pe is derived from the Egyptian ro, but it denotes p, not r, because pe is the Phoenician for 'mouth'.

4. *The Greek alphabet.*   Some time after 1000 B.C. the Phoenician alphabet was taken over by the Ionic-speaking Greeks settled on the Aegean coast of Anatolia. The Phoenician origin of the Greek alphabet

is shown both by the names of the letters, derived from the Phoenician names, and by the letters themselves, which bear in most cases a recognisable resemblance to their Phoenician originals (Table III). Among the Phoenician signs were several representing consonants which did not exist in Greek. These were used for the vowels. During the colonial expansion of the Greeks in the eighth and seventh centuries B.C. the alphabet developed in a number of local varieties, which fall into two main groups, East Greek and West Greek. The East Greek group includes the Attic, which later became the standard form of the Greek alphabet. The West Greek, current in Italy and Sicily, was transmitted to the Etruscans and through them to the Romans. Most of the differences between the Latin (Roman) and Greek (Attic) alphabets are either derived from differences between the East and West Greek alphabets or due to changes introduced by the Etruscans and Romans in adapting the West Greek alphabet to their own languages. The most important of them are explained in the next chapter. The Greeks of Cyprus continued to use a pre-alphabetic script, known as the Cypriot syllabary, down to the third century B.C.

V. PHONOLOGY

1. *AG phonology*. The principal phonological characteristics of AG are: the preservation, in a modified form, of the IE accentual system, based on pitch; a tendency to move the vowels forward from the back to the front of the mouth; the loss of initial s- before vowels and of medial -s- between vowels; and the weakening of final consonants, leaving only -s -n -r. This chapter should be studied together with Tables III and IV.

2. *Simple vowels*. AG A and I may be either long or short, as in Latin (Eng. bath but, French dire dit). So originally was E, but in Ionic and Attic it became confined to short e (Eng. let) as opposed to H, which represented long open e (French tête). The history of H is as follows. In the earliest form of the Greek alphabet it had denoted the aspirate (Eng. *h*it), and it retained this value in the West Greek and Latin alphabets. But in the E. Ionic dialect, for which the Greek alphabet was originally designed, the aspirate disappeared; and so this letter became redundant. In the same period Ionic and Attic evolved a new vowel, a long flat e (Eng. drag), derived from PG ā. The letter H was used to represent this new vowel (Texts 1). Subsequently, however, this long flat e

became assimilated to long open e (French tête) and the value of H changed accordingly. E had originally denoted a closed e, short or long (Eng. let late); subsequently the long form was written EI, which also denoted the diphthong ei. O had originally denoted a closed o, short or long (Eng. cargo, bowl), and also a long open o (Eng. bore). Later, it was restricted to short closed o; the corresponding long vowel was written OY, and the long open o was written Ω. Later still, in Attic, the combination ου acquired the value ū (Eng. boot). The letter Y had originally the value u, long or short (Eng. boot book), but in Attic it became equivalent to French u (German ü). Hence the Latin Y, introduced to denote this sound in words borrowed from Greek. In HG the diphthong οι acquired the same value; hence the name ὒ ψιλόν (upsilon 'simple υ') to distinguish υ from οι. New names were also invented for ε, ο, ω: ἒ ψιλόν (epsilon 'simple ε') to distinguish it from αι, which in HG acquired the same value; ὂ μικρόν (omikron 'little o') and ὢ μέγα (omega 'big o'), which in HG became phonetically identical, as in MG.

3. *Diphthongs.* Followed by ι, the simple vowels yielded the following diphthongs: αι ᾱι, ει ηι, οι ωι, υι (French oui). Where the first vowel was long (ᾱι ηι ωι), the ι ceased to be pronounced or written in HG, but in BG it was restored in writing as the 'iota subscript' (ᾳ ῃ ῳ) without affecting the pronunciation. Followed by υ (which in these diphthongs retained its original value u), the simple vowels yielded the diphthongs αυ (Eng. how), ευ (Eng. let + lute), ηυ (Eng. late + lute).

4. *Simple consonants.* The letters Β Δ Κ Λ Μ Ν Π Ρ Σ Τ had approximately the same value in AG as in Latin and English. Γ corresponds to Latin G, which is a modified form of C. (In early Latin there was some confusion between C, K and Q, due probably to the influence of Etruscan; after the introduction of G, C acquired the value of K, which accordingly disappeared). The AG equivalent of Latin F was Ϝ, (δίγαμμα, i.e. 'double gamma', so called from its shape) which survived in several dialects, but not in Attic-Ionic: it had the value of English w. The letters Θ Φ Χ represented aspirated stops (Eng. hothouse uphill workhouse) which in Latin words borrowed from Greek were written TH PH CH.

5. *Double consonants.* The letters Ζ Ξ Ψ represented double consonants: dz (earlier zd), ks, ps; in Latin they were written Z X PS. The Latin X is the same letter as the Greek X. The difference in value may be explained on the hypothesis that, when the East and West Greek alphabets diverged, the value of this sign was not yet fixed. Other double consonants are (1) κκ, λλ, μμ, νν; (2) γγ, γκ, γχ; (3) σσ ττ. In the first group the simple consonant is heard twice (Eng. all late, sheep pen,

in need). In the second group the γ sounds as ng (Eng. anger, canker, sank her). The combinations σσ and ττ represented in CG some such sounds as Eng. sh ch (sash such) but in HG they acquired the value of double s and double t respectively. In the other double consonants (μβ μπ μφ νδ ντ νθ etc.) each letter had its proper value.

6. *Breathings.* Every word beginning with a vowel carries over its first syllable (over the first letter, if it is a simple vowel, or over the second letter, if it is a diphthong) a sign called a breathing, which exists in two forms, the rough breathing (ʻ) and the smooth breathing (ʼ). The rough breathing denoted the presence, and the smooth breathing the absence, of an initial aspiration. These two signs, formed by dividing vertically the letter H (Ⱶ ⱶ), were introduced into Attic and other dialects after the letter H, which had originally denoted the aspirate, had been transferred to long open e. Initial ρ (derived in many cases from *hr-) was always written with the rough breathing. For the accents see VI.4.

VI. INFLECTION AND ACCENTUATION

1. *Inflection.* An inflection is an element in the structure of a word, occurring usually but not always at the end, which determines the syntactical relation of that word to the other words in the sentence. The inflections of the noun and pronoun are called cases. An inflected language is one in which the principle of inflection is highly developed; an uninflected language is one in which there are few or no inflections. Ancient Greek and Latin are inflected languages, because in them the noun, pronoun and verb are all highly inflected. So is Modern Greek, but less so than Ancient Greek. In English, which has lost nearly all its inflections, syntactical relations are determined partly by the use of separate words and partly by the order of words in the sentence. For example, the English future contains three elements: the pronoun, marking the person and number; the auxiliary verb, marking the tense; and the main verb: 'I shall say'. These elements are separable and their order is variable: 'I shall not say', 'shall I say?'. The Greek verb also contains three elements, representing the verb stem, the tense, and the person and number (φή·σ·ω); but they are inseparable and their order is fixed. The difference between the statement ('I shall say') and the question ('shall I say?') is indicated in Greek by the use of interrogative particles (ᾱρα φήσω;). The inflectional system of Greek, as of other IE languages, is derived from Common Indo-European. It is probable that the IE

inflections originated as independent words, which gradually lost their independence and became suffixes and later still were absorbed into the words to which they were attached: AG εἰμί (Aeolic ἐμμί) from PG *ἐσ-μι, IE *es-mi, i.e. 'is me'; Latin Romā, Old Latin Romād, i.e. Romā-d, cf. de 'from'.

2. *Word-order.* In English, the syntactical relations of the words in a sentence are determined mainly by their position: 'Achilles killed Hector'. In Greek, however, owing to the use of inflections, the order of words may be varied without altering their syntactical relations: Ἕκτορα ἀπέκτεινεν Ἀχιλλεύς, Ἀχιλλεὺς ἀπέκτεινεν Ἕκτορα. In Greek the word-order is used to mark the emphasis, the emphatic word being placed at or near the beginning of the sentence or clause. In English, for the reason given, the word-order is much less flexible. This is a fundamental difference between the two languages.

3. *Accent.* There are two kinds of accent, stress and pitch (or tone). A syllable carrying a stress accent is spoken with greater force than the others; a syllable carrying a pitch accent is spoken on a higher or lower musical note. A strong stress accent tends to obscure the quality of the unstressed vowels, as in English; a pitch accent does not have this effect. Both stress and pitch are present in English, as in MG, but stress predominates. In AG there was, so far as we know, only pitch. Each kind of accent may be a function of the word or of the sentence or of both. The English stress is primarily a function of the word: every word, except some monosyllables, normally carries on one of its syllables a stress, which is an integral part of it. The English pitch is a function of the sentence, that is, the accentuation of the sentence is varied by pitch according to the sense: 'Enough?' 'Enough!' The AG pitch was a function of the word. Every word, with certain exceptions, carried on one syllable a pitch, which was an integral part of the word. Consequently, the accentuation of the sentence was less flexible in AG than it is in English, being fixed by the accentuation of the individual words. This is another fundamental difference between the two languages. We may say that, while the order of words is fixed in English, being determined by their syntactical relations, and free in Greek, the sentence accent is fixed in Greek, being determined by the accentuation of the individual words, and free in English—free, that is, to mark degrees of emphasis and other shades of meaning as distinct from syntactical relations. In AG such shades of meaning were conveyed partly by the word-order and partly by modal particles: (1) 'You were in town' Tu étais en ville ἐν ἄστει γὰρ ἦσθα, (2) '*You* were in town?' Toi, tu étais en ville? ἦ καὶ σὺ ἦσθ' ἐν ἄστει;

(3) 'You *were* in town' Tu étais bien en ville ἦσθ' ἄρ' ἐν ἄστει, (4) 'You were in *town*' C'est en ville que tu étais ἐν ἄστει γὰρ δήπου ἦσθα. It will be seen that from this point of view AG is closer to French than to English.

4. *The Greek accents*.   AG had three accentual signs: (1) the acute, denoting a rising tone, (2) the circumflex, denoting a rising-falling tone, and (3) the grave, denoting a falling tone or in some cases simply the absence of an acute. Generally speaking, the acute was restricted to the last three syllables of the word, and to the last two if the final was long; the circumflex to the last two syllables, and to the final if it was long; and the grave to the final syllable. A word carrying an acute accent on its final syllable lost it (replaced in writing by a grave) when followed without a pause by another accented word: καλὸς ἀνήρ, ἀνὴρ καλός. Certain words, mostly monosyllables, carried no accent themselves but threw back an acute accent on to the final syllable of the preceding word: δίκαιός τις ἀνήρ, ἠκούσαμέν τινος, ὧδέ πως. These words are called enclitics. After pitch had given way to stress, the ancient accents were retained in writing to mark the stressed syllable.

5. *Quantity*.   The quantity of a syllable is the relative length of time required to pronounce it, which varies according to the length of the vowel and the number of consonants it contains. Quantity exists in English (set sate sets sates skates) but has no functional value. In AG every syllable was treated conventionally as either long or short, and this distinction served as the rhythmical basis of poetry like the distinction between stressed and unstressed syllables in English. Every simple vowel had both a long form and a short form ('natural' quantity); double vowels (diphthongs) were generally treated as long, and so also were simple vowels, short by nature, when followed by two or more consonants ('positional' quantity).

VII. THE NOUN

1. *Substantive and adjective*.   The noun includes both substantive and adjective, which in function are to large extent interchangeable ('the pure in heart', 'a sailor man') and in form have a common system of inflections.

2. *Gender*.   The Greek noun has three genders: masculine, feminine, neuter. This system goes back to Common Indo-European. It is believed to have originated in the personal pronouns, from which it was extended

by analogy to the adjective and later to the substantive. Further, there are indications that the IE system of three genders had been superimposed on an earlier system of two classes, animate and inanimate. The animate class included beings or things which were alive or believed to be alive and could therefore be regarded as agents; the inanimate class included inanimate objects, which could be acted on but could not act. This explains why the neuter gender (corresponding to the inanimate class) has no distinctive ending for the nominative case. The idea of gender was probably in origin a projection of the division of the community into men, women and children. The masculine and feminine were formed as subdivisions of the animate class. The masculine was reserved originally for male beings or things which were regarded as having male functions, e.g. the sky, as the source of rain, and rivers, as fertilising agents. The feminine was reserved in the same way for female beings and things, e.g. the earth and trees, which bear fruit. The association of the neuter with children, which, being sexually immature, were regarded as sexless, may be seen in such words for child as AG τέκνον and German Kind, which are neuter, and in the use of the neuter for the formation of diminutives. In all the IE languages, as we know them, distinctions of gender have become for the most part purely formal categories. and in some they have been reduced to two or have entirely disappeared.

3. *Case.* Eight cases can be traced in the IE languages: (1) the nominative, denoting the agent (grammatical subject); (2) the vocative, used in direct address; (3) the accusative, denoting (a) the goal of motion or (b) the object to which the action of the verb is directed (grammatical object); (4) the genitive, denoting origin, dependence, or possession; (5) the dative, denoting the indirect object of the verb; (6) the ablative, denoting separation; (7) the locative, denoting location; (8) the instrumental, denoting the instrument with which the action of the verb is effected. The vocative is strictly speaking not a case at all. A noun in the vocative is an exclamation, standing in no syntactical relation to the rest of the sentence. That is why in Greek the vocative consists normally of the plain stem without a case-ending.

4. *The Greek cases.* AG had five cases, the ablative being merged with the genitive, the locative and instrumental with the dative. MG has four, the dative being merged with the genitive. The reduction in the number of cases led to overloading of those that survived, and hence to the development of prepositions, which were originally adverbs designed to reinforce the case-endings; and, once established, the use of prepositions tended to reduce still further the number of cases by rendering the case-

endings superfluous: AG εἰς τὸν ἥλιον, ἀπὸ τοῦ ἡλίου MG εἰς τὸν ἥλιον, ἀπὸ τὸν ἥλιον. The process may be illustrated by the example given above (VI.1): Old Latin Romā-d, Classical Latin Romā, Late Latin de Roma, French de Rome.

5. *Secondary uses of the cases.* Besides the primary uses mentioned above, the AG cases developed a number of secondary uses, of which the most important are the following. The accusative was used to mark the extent, spatial or temporal, of the action of the verb: μακρὰν ὁδὸν ἰέναι 'to go a long way', ἀλγεῖν τοὺς πόδας 'to have sore feet', μακρὸν χρόνον πορεύεσθαι 'to travel a long time'. The true genitive was used spatially to denote the part of a whole (partitive genitive): ἐλάβετο τῆς μητρὸς τὸ παιδίον 'the child caught hold of its mother', cf. ἔλαβε τὸ παιδίον ἡ μήτηρ 'the mother took the child'. Temporally it was used to denote a point of time falling within an extended period: ὀλίγον πρότερον τῆς νυκτός 'a little earlier in the night'. The ablatival genitive was used to express comparison: ἐμοῦ μικρότερός ἐστι 'he is smaller than I' ('he is on the small side from me'); hence the so-called 'genitive absolute' construction: θεοῦ θέλοντος σωθήσεται 'he will be saved, God willing' ('starting from God being willing...'). The locatival dative was used to mark the moment of the action of the verb (a usage which stands to the accusative of extent in the same relation as the perfective to the imperfective aspect of the verb): τῇ ὑστεραίᾳ ἀφίκοντο 'they came the next day'. The instrumental dative was used to express manner and measure: δρόμῳ ἀπῆλθον 'they went off at a run', τοσούτῳ χαλεπώτερον 'so much the more difficult'.

6. *Prepositions.* The primary function of prepositions, in Greek as in other languages, was to express spatial relations; later, they were extended to temporal relations, time being expressed in terms of motion, and later still to other abstract relations: διὰ δώματα 'through the rooms', διὰ τὴν νύκτα 'through the night', δι' ἄγνοιαν 'through ignorance'. See Table XV.

7. *Number.* AG had three numbers—singular, plural and dual. The dual was an old IE category, reflecting the division of the primitive tribe into two moieties. In AG it had only two case-endings for the noun, nominative-vocative-accusative and genitive-dative (Table VI. 23), and two persons for the verb, second and third (Table IX.39). Its use was confined mainly to things that go in pairs, like hands, eyes, ears, twins etc. It lasted longest in Attic but disappeared in HG.

VIII. THE VERB

1. *Voice.* The AG verb has three voices: active, middle, passive. The active voice expresses a simple action, either transitive (with an object) or intransitive (without an object), or a process. The middle voice is a reflexive, either direct ('I wash myself') or indirect ('wash something for myself', e.g. 'I wash my hands'). From its use as a direct reflexive the middle voice of transitive verbs developed two further functions: (1) intransitive ('I wash', sc. myself) and (2) passive ('I am washed'). In Greek, as in other languages, the passive voice was a relatively late development. There are no distinctively passive endings. In the present, imperfect, perfect and pluperfect, and in the future of some verbs, the passive forms are identical with the middle forms and may be described as medio-passive. In the future of other verbs the endings are those of the middle but they are preceded by the infix -θη-. The aorist passive is in origin an intransitive aorist active. Its endings are those of the athematic aorist active, preceded by the infix -θε-/-θη- ('weak' aorist passive) or -ε-/-η- ('strong' aorist passive). Finally, from its use as an indirect reflexive ('I do something for myself') the middle voice of transitive verbs came to denote a mediated action ('I get something done'): γράφω ἐπιστολήν 'I write a letter' (active), γράφομαι ἐπιστολήν 'I get a letter written' (middle).

2. *Mood.* The Greek verb has four moods: indicative, subjunctive, optative, imperative. The primary functions of these moods may be defined as follows. They were used to denote respectively expressions of (1) fact, (2) intention, (3) possibility, (4) command. The indicative is the mood for direct statements of fact: ἴμεν 'we are going'. The subjunctive expresses primarily either an intention regarding the immediate future or a wish whose fulfilment lies within the speaker's control: ἴομεν (Attic ἴωμεν) 'we will go', 'let us go'. The optative expresses a possibility or a wish whose fulfilment lies outside the speaker's control: ἴοιμεν 'may we go', 'if only we might go!'. It will be seen that these differences of meaning correspond to the differences of form: ἴ-μεν, ἴ-ο-μεν, ἴ-ο-ι-μεν. The first is the mood of actuality; the second is one degree removed from actuality (immediate or volitional future); the third is two degrees removed from actuality (potential future). The imperative is the mood of command. In the second person singular it consists of the plain stem without an ending, like the vocative case of the noun (VII.3) and for the same reason: it was in origin an exclamation, without syntactical relations. The moods are categories of the finite

verb, that is, of the verb as constituting a complete sentence.

3. *Tense.* The tenses are categories marking distinctions of time. The AG verb has six tenses: present, future, imperfect, aorist, perfect, pluperfect. The imperfect and pluperfect tenses exist only in the indicative mood. The present and future indicative denote present and future actions. The imperfect denotes a past action, either incomplete ('I was going') or repeated ('I used to go'). The aorist indicative denotes a past action regarded as complete ('I went'). The perfect denoted originally the state corresponding to the action of the verb, and this usage survived in some verbs: ἐγείρω 'I wake' (transitive), ἐγρήγορα 'I am awake'. But in general it was used to denote a present state resulting from a past action: ἀκήκοα ('I have heard'). The pluperfect is the perfect projected into past time: 'I was awake', 'I had heard'.

4. *Aspect.* The aspect of a verb relates not to the time of the action but to the point of view from which it is regarded by the speaker. Thus, distinctions of tense are objective, while distinctions of aspect are subjective. In the Greek verb as we know it distinctions of tense predominate over distinctions of aspect, but the latter are very important. In the IE verb aspect had predominated over tense. In the Greek verb we find traces of several aspects (imperfective—'I am going'; perfective—'I go'; frequentative—'I go every day'; conative—'I am trying to go'; inceptive— 'I start to go'); but the most clearly distinguished are the first two. In the imperfective aspect the action of the verb is regarded as a process, that is, either as a single action extended in time or as a series of repeated actions; in the perfective aspect the action is regarded as complete. The English verb distinguishes these two aspects in all tenses: 'I go', 'I am going'; 'I shall go', 'I shall be going'; 'I went', 'I was going', 'I used to go'; 'I have gone', 'I have been going'; 'I had gone', 'I had been going'. In the AG verb they are not distinguished in the present and future indicative, but the imperfect and aorist indicative might be regarded from this point of view as a single (past) tense divided into two (imperfective and perfective) aspects. In the non-indicative moods there are no tense distinctions at all, except in the future. The difference in meaning between the present and aorist forms of the subjunctive, optative and imperative is simply that the present forms are imperfective, and the aorist forms perfective: present imperative πῖνε 'go on drinking'; aorist imperative πίε 'drink it up!'.

5. *The future tense.* In Greek, as in other languages, the future was a comparatively late development, being in origin a subjective or volitional future and so closely related to the subjunctive. AG (Attic) ὦ (Epic

ἔω), from *ἔσω, subjunctive of the verb 'to be', is the same word as the Latin ero, future of the verb 'to be'; and so in Epic the subjunctive is often used as a future.

6. *The augment.*   Past time is indicated by a prefix (ἐ-) used with the imperfect, aorist and pluperfect indicative. This prefix, called the augment, is pre-Greek, being found also in Sanskrit, but it did not become fully established until the beginning of the historical period. In Epic it is present or absent according to metrical convenience. In verbs compounded with a preposition it is placed between the preposition and the verb stem. Where the verb stem begins with a vowel, the two vowels contract: see Table XII.7-8.

7. *Reduplication.*   The formation of words by reduplication is a very primitive phenomenon, found in virtually all languages. It was highly developed in the IE verb and survived in AG in the present, aorist and perfect. In many verbs the present stem was formed by reduplication from the simple stem, which was usually preserved in the aorist. The reduplicated aorists are for the most part confined to Epic. It survived most fully, however, as a sign of the perfect tense, which in almost all verbs is reduplicated. In a few perfects the stem is reduplicated in full (ἐγρήγορα) but in most verbs beginning with a single consonant other than σ- the reduplicator consists of that consonant plus ε (λέλυκα). Where the verb stem begins with a double consonant, the reduplicator usually consists simply of ἐ-, formed on the analogy of the augment (ἔσπαρκα, cf. ἔσχηκα from *ἐσχηκα from *σεσχηκα).

8. *Person and number.*   The AG verb has three persons and three numbers, except that there is no first person dual. When the subject of the sentence is a noun in the neuter plural, the verb is in the third person singular. This is because the neuter plural ending -α was originally the feminine singular of a collective noun.

9. *Sequence.*   The finite verb has a set of six basic personal endings (singular and plural) which appear in two forms or sequences, primary and secondary. The primary sequence is used in the present, future and perfect indicative, and in the subjunctive; the secondary sequence is used in the imperfect, aorist and pluperfect indicative, and in the optative. See Table IX A.

10. *The infinitive and participle.*   The infinitive is a verbal substantive; the participle is a verbal adjective (I.8). The basic endings of the infinitive are -εν (-ειν), -μεν, -ναι (active) and -σθαι (middle). The participle is formed with the elements -ντ- and -οτ- (active) and -μεν- (middle). See Table X.

IX. VOWEL GRADATION

1. *Vowel gradation* (Ablaut) is the alternation of vowels in nouns and verbs belonging to a common root: sing sang sung song. The alternating vowel is called the theme-vowel. Where the theme-vowel forms part of the stem, we speak of radical vowel gradation: λόγ-ος (omikron grade), λέγ-ω (epsilon grade) λείπ-ω (epsilon grade); λέ·λοιπ-α (omikron grade). Where the theme-vowel occurs after the stem and before the ending (if there is an ending), we speak of post-radical vowel gradation: λόγ-ος (omikron grade), λόγ-ε (epsilon grade), λόγ-ον (omikron grade); λέγ-ο·μεν (omikron grade), λέγ-ε·τε (epsilon grade). Further examples: πατέρα πατρί ἀπάτορα, λείπω ἔλιπον. It will be observed that in the forms πατρί and ἔλιπον the stem is characterised by the absence of a theme-vowel: this is called the zero grade. The commonest type of vowel gradation consists of these three grades, but we also find another type, based on a single vowel (long and short grade); φημί (< φᾱμί) φαμέν.

2. *Radical vowel gradation* appears in nouns and verbs and in substantives and adjectives formed from the same root: λόγ·ος λέγ·ω, πατέρ·α ἀπάτορ·α. In some verbs, called strong verbs, it serves to distinguish the present, aorist and perfect: λείπω ἔλιπον λέλοιπα. In some presents (athematic) and perfects it marks the distinction between singular and plural: φη·μί (< φᾱ·μί) φα·μέν, γέ·γον·α γέ·γα·μεν (< *γε·γν·μεν, Att. γεγόναμεν).

3. *Post-radical vowel gradation.* Nouns subject to post-radical vowel gradation contain three elements (stem, theme-vowel, ending) and are called thematic nouns: λόγ·ο·ς λόγ·ε λόγ·ο·ν. (The vocative consists of stem and theme-vowel only, without an ending: see VII.3). The nouns in -ᾱ (-η) belong to this type, though in these the gradation has left only a few traces: Ep. νύμφη (nom.), νύμφα (voc.) from nom. νύμφᾱ, voc. νύμφα. Nouns without post-radical vowel gradation contain only two elements (stem and ending) and are called athematic nouns: παῖ·ς (< *παιδ·ς), παῖ (< *παιδ), παῖδα (<* παιδν). (The vocative παῖ consists of the stem only). Verbs are classified in the same way: thematic ἴ·ο·μεν δύ·ο·μεν, athematic ἴ·μεν ἔ·δυ·μεν. Every verb contains both thematic and athematic forms. The future and subjunctive are always thematic; the perfect medio-passive is always athematic. In noun and verb alike the athematic type is the older.

4. *The three aorists.* There are three types of aorist active and middle: athematic (ἔ·δυ·ν ἐ·δύ·μην), thematic (ἔ·λιπ·ο·ν ἐ·λιπ·ό·μην), sigmatic (ἔ·δυ·σα ἐ·δυ·σά·μην). The sigmatic aorist was formed from the athematic

aorist by inserting the infix -σ-. In those verbs which have both an athematic and a sigmatic aorist active, the former is intransitive and the latter transitive: ἔδυ τὸ πλοῖον 'the boat sank', ἔδυσε τὸ πλοῖον 'he sank the boat'. The distinction between the thematic aorist and the sigmatic aorist is purely formal, and, where both forms are found in the same verb, they have the same meaning, the thematic being the older: ἔπιθον ἔπεισα, ἐπιθόμην ἐπεισάμην.

5. *Origin of vowel gradation.* It is believed that the IE system of vowel gradation goes back to a stage of Common IE at which the accent contained an element of stress, and that the gradation arose from the qualitative difference between stressed and unstressed vowels, cf. Sanskrit émi imáḥ, AG εἶμι ἴμες ἴμεν (for *ἰμές *ἰμέν). In the IE languages as we know them it is a purely formal system; but it must at one time have had a functional value, which indeed survives to some extent in AG: λεῖπε λίπε, λείπω λίπω, ἔλειπον ἔλιπον. The structure of some archaic AG verbs suggests that it had at one time been used to mark distinctions of aspect: athematic ἴ·μεν (imperfective) 'we are going'; thematic ἴ·ο·μεν (perfective, later subjunctive) 'we go', i.e. 'we will go' (immediate volitional future), 'let us go' (VIII.2).

X. SYNTAX

1. *The simple sentence.* The simplest form of the verbal sentence consists in Greek of a finite verb inflected in the proper manner: καθεύδει 'he's asleep'. Similarly, the simplest form of the nominal sentence consists of two nouns juxtaposed, the predicate being usually placed first: AG χρήματ᾽ ἀνήρ 'man is money', πάντων μέτρον ἄνθρωπος 'man is the measure of all things', MG παθήματα μαθήματα 'sufferings are lessons'. In such sentences Attic normally distinguishes the subject by using the article with it: πολλὰ τὰ δεινά 'wonders are many', ἄτοπον τὸ ἐνύπνιον 'it is a queer dream'. The copula was introduced in order to express distinctions of tense and mood: τὸ δέ τοι ξεινήιον ἔσται 'that shall be your gift', ταῦτ᾽ ἂν εἴη βλαβερά 'that would be harmful'. When the verb ἐστί is used as a full word, it carries an accent and comes first: ἔστιν ὁ θεός 'God is', ἔστι πόλις 'there is a city', ἔστι ταῦτα 'that is so'.

2. *The compound sentence.* The principle of subordination was developed from the practice of using two simple sentences together in such a way that one was subordinated to the other, first in meaning and later in form. The more primitive practice is still current in colloquial speech: 'Say one

word more, and I'll box your ears'. So in Greek: τί θέλετέ μοι δοῦναι, κἀγὼ ὑμῖν παραδώσω αὐτόν; 'what are you willing to give me, and I will deliver him unto you?' (i.e. 'what will you give me, if I deliver him unto you?'). Hence: φοβοῦμαι μὴ πέσῃ 'I'm afraid (lest) he may fall' ('I'm afraid—let him not fall!'); ἔνθα δὲ Σίσυφος ἔσκεν, ὃ κέρδιστος γένετ' ἀνδρῶν 'And there was Sisyphos, who was the most covetous of men' ('he was the most covetous of men'); ἀλλ' ἴθι, μή μ' ἐρέθιζε, σαώτερος ὥς κε νέηαι 'go, don't provoke me, so that you may go the more safely' ('so you will go the more safely'). Thus, the evolution of the compound sentence may be compared with the evolution of the inflected word (VI.1).

3. *Conjunctions.* The subordinate clause is attached to the principal clause by means of a relative pronoun or adverb or by a conjunction, that is, a particle which serves this structural function and at the same time indicates the nature of the relation between the two clauses. The AG relative pronoun ὅς ἥ ὅ was in origin a demonstrative—a function which it preserved in Epic; the conjunction ὅτι 'that' 'because' is properly the acc.sg.n. of the indefinite relative ὅστις; other conjunctions were derived from adverbs or demonstrative pronouns, e.g. πρίν 'before', εἰ αἰ < *e·i *a·i (the locative case of a demonstrative pronoun, 'there' 'then' 'so'); ὅπως ὅπου etc. were probably modelled on ὅτι.

4. *The negative particles.* AG had two negatives, οὐ (οὐκ before an unaspirated vowel, οὐχ before an aspirated vowel, also οὐχί) and μή. The first is objective, being used for negative statements of fact; the second is subjective, being used for negative commands (prohibitions), wishes and conditions: (1) οὐκ ἀκούεις 'you are not listening'; μὴ ἄκουε 'don't listen'; (2) τοῦ πατρὸς ἐμνήσθη, ὃν οὔποτ' εἶδον 'he mentioned his father, whom I never saw'; ἃ μὴ οἶδα, οὐδὲ οἴομαι εἰδέναι, 'I don't think I know what I don't know'; (3) οἱ οὐ παρόντες 'those who are not present' (referring to particular persons); οἱ μὴ παρόντες 'those who are not present' (whoever they may be); (4) τὸ μὴ λέγειν 'not to speak'; τὸ οὐ λέγειν 'the fact of not speaking'. When one of these simple negatives is accompanied by a compound negative, the negation is either intensified or cancelled, according as the simple form precedes or follows the compound form: οὐκ ἦλθεν οὐδείς 'nobody came'; οὐδεὶς οὐκ ἦλθε 'there was nobody who did not come'.

5. *Classification of subordinate clauses.* The following sentences taken from Plato's *Symposium* are arranged according to I.15-18. The MG renderings are from the translation by D. Photiadis.

(a) Substantival clauses

(1) Subject clauses

173c Οὐκ ἄξιον περὶ τούτων, 'Απολλόδωρε, νῦν ἐρίζειν. 'It is not worth while to dispute that now'. Δὲν ἀξίζει, 'Απολλόδωρε, νὰ φιλονεικήσουμε γιὰ τέτοιο πρᾶμα τώρα.

177a Οὐ δεινόν, φησίν, ὦ 'Ερυξίμαχε, ἄλλοις μέν τισι θεῶν ὕμνους καὶ παιῶνας εἶναι ὑπὸ τῶν ποιητῶν πεποιημένους, τῷ δ' "Ερωτι, τηλικούτῳ ὄντι καὶ τοσούτῳ θεῷ, μηδ' ἕνα πώποτε τοσούτων γεγονότων ποιητῶν πεποιηκέναι μηδὲν ἐγκώμιον; 'Isn't it a shocking thing, Eryximachos, that, though hymns and paeans have been composed by the poets to other gods, not a single one of them has ever made a eulogy for a god so venerable and powerful as Love?'. Δὲν εἶναι τρομερό, 'Ερυξίμαχε, νὰ ἔχουν φτιάξει οἱ ποιητὲς γιὰ ἄλλους θεοὺς ὕμνους καὶ παιᾶνες, καὶ τὸν "Ερωτα, ποὺ εἶναι τόσο γέρος καὶ μεγάλος θεός, νὰ μὴν ἔχει βρεθεῖ οὔτε ἕνας ἀπ' ὅλο αὐτὸ τὸ πλῆθος τῶν ποιητῶν νὰ τὸν ἐγκωμιάσει;

(2) Object clauses

172b "Εφη δὲ καὶ σὲ εἰδέναι. 'He said you knew too'. Εἶπε πὼς τὸ ξέρεις κ' ἐσύ.

173a 'Αλλ' εἰπέ μοι πότε ἐγένετο ἡ συνουσία αὕτη; 'Tell me when this party took place'. Καὶ πές μου πότε ἔγινε αὐτὸ τὸ γλέντι.

173d Καὶ ἴσως αὖ ὑμεῖς ἐμὲ ἡγεῖσθε κακοδαίμονα εἶναι, καὶ οἶμαι ὑμᾶς ἀληθῆ οἴεσθαι. 'Perhaps you think I am a miserable wretch—I daresay you are right'. Μπορεῖ βέβαια νὰ νομίζετε ἐσεῖς πὼς ἐγὼ εἶμαι ἀξιολύπητος, κ' ἴσως νὰ ἔχετε δίκιο.

(b) Adjectival clauses

178a Πάντων μὲν οὖν ἃ ἕκαστος εἶπεν, οὔτε πάνυ ὁ 'Αριστόδημος ἐμέμνητο οὔτ' αὖ ἐγὼ ἃ ἐκεῖνος ἔλεγεν. 'Aristodemos did not remember all that everybody said, nor do I remember all he told me'. Τὰ ὅσα εἶπε ὁ καθένας τους, οὔτε ὁ 'Αριστόδημος βέβαια τὰ θυμόταν καλά, οὔτε πάλι ἐγὼ ὅλα ὅσα μοῦ διηγήθηκε.

(c) Adverbial clauses

(1) Final

174a Ταῦτα δὴ ἐκαλλωπισάμην, ἵνα καλὸς πρὸς καλὸν ἴω. 'I have dressed up like this in order to be a handsome visitor for a handsome host'. Στολίστηκα λοιπόν, γιὰ νὰ πάω ὡραῖος σὲ ὡραῖον.

(2) Consecutive

192d Εἰ γὰρ τούτου ἐπιθυμεῖτε, θέλω ὑμᾶς συντῆξαι καὶ συμφυσῆσαι εἰς τὸ αὐτό, ὥστε δύο ὄντας ἕνα γεγονέναι. 'If that is what you desire, I am willing to melt you and weld you into each other, so that the two of you will become one'. "Αν αὐτὸ ἐπιθυμεῖτε, εἶμαι ἔτοιμος νὰ λειώσω καὶ νὰ χύσω τὸν καθένα σας μέσα στὸν ἄλλον, ἔτσι ποὺ ἀπὸ δύο ποὺ εἴσαστε νὰ σᾶς κάνω ἕναν.

(3) Concessive

212e Ἐγὼ δέ, κἂν ὑμεῖς γελᾶτε, ὅμως εὖ οἶδ' ὅτι ἀληθῆ λέγω. 'Though you may laugh, I know I am telling the truth'. Ἐγὼ ὅμως ξέρω καλά, κι ἂς με περιγελᾶτε ἐσεῖς, πὼς μιλῶ σωστά.

(4) Causal

180d Ἐπεὶ δὲ δὴ δύο ἐστόν ('Αφροδίτα), δύο ἀνάγκη καὶ "Ερωτε εἶναι. 'Since there are two Aphrodites, there must be two Loves as well'. Μά, καθὼς δύο εἶναι οἱ 'Αφροδίτες, ἀναγκαστικὰ δύο εἶναι κ' οἱ "Ερωτες.

(5) Modal

193d "Ωσπερ οὖν κατεδεήθην σου, μὴ κωμῳδήσῃς αὐτόν. 'As I begged you, don't make fun of it'. Μά, καθὼς σὲ παρακάλεσα, μὴ τὴν κοροϊδέψεις.

(6) Temporal

203b "Οτε γὰρ ἐγένετο ἡ 'Αφροδίτη, ἡστιῶντο οἱ θεοί. 'When Aphrodite was born, the gods were feasting.' "Οταν γεννήθηκε ἡ 'Αφροδίτη, γλεντοκοποῦσαν οἱ θεοί.

(7) Local

194a Εἰ δὲ γένοιο οὗ νῦν ἐγώ εἰμι, . . . καὶ μάλ' ἂν φοβοῖο. 'If you were in my position, you certainly would be alarmed'. "Αν ὅμως τύχαινε νὰ ἤσουνα στὴ θέση ποὺ εἶμαι, . . . καὶ πάρα πολὺ θ' ἀνησυχοῦσες.

(8) Conditional

188e "Η εἴ πως ἄλλως ἐν νῷ ἔχεις ἐγκωμιάζειν τὸν θεόν, ἐγκωμίαζε. 'Or if you intend to praise him in some other way, do so'. "Αν τυχὸν λογαριάζεις διαφορετικὰ νὰ ἐγκωμιάσεις τὸν θεό, παίνα τον.

215b Ἐὰν γὰρ μὴ ὁμολογήσῃς, μάρτυρας παρέξομαι. 'If you don't admit it, I will call witnesses'. "Αν δὲν τὸ παραδεχτῆς, θὰ φέρω μάρτυρες.

195c Οὐ γὰρ ἂν ἐκτομαὶ οὐδὲ δεσμοὶ ἀλλήλων ἐγίγνοντο καὶ ἄλλα πολλὰ βίαια, εἰ "Ερως ἐν αὐτοῖς ἦν. 'If Love had been among them, there would not have been all those mutilations and incarcerations and other acts of violence'. "Αν ἦταν τότε ἀνάμεσά τους αὐτός, οὔτε ἀκρωτηριασμοὶ θὰ γίνονταν οὔτε ἀλυσοδέματα, οὔτε ὅλες οἱ ἄλλες οἱ βίες.

XI. PREHISTORIC GREEK

1. *Greek and Armenian.*   The language most closely related to Greek is Armenian, but they are not close enough to be classed together in one group. One of the distinctive features they have in common is the use of prothetic vowels: Greek με ἐμέ, Armenian im (from *ime), Latin me; Greek ὄνομα, Armenian anun, Latin nomen; Greek ἄστρον, Armenian astl, Latin stella. It may be that they are descended from a particular

dialect of Common IE. After Armenian, the languages nearest to Greek are the Indo-Iranian and the Italic.

2. *Other Aegean languages.* Greek was introduced gradually into the Aegean basin by a series of immigrations extending over most of the second millennium B.C. During this period the dominant powers in the Aegean were, first, Minoan Crete, with its capital at Knossos, which was probably not Greek-speaking, at least not before the fifteenth century B.C., and later, Mycenae, which probably was Greek-speaking. We possess many inscriptions of this period, not yet satisfactorily deciphered, and also an inscription from Lemnos in a language resembling Etruscan, which was introduced to Italy by emigrants from Lydia. This may have been the language of the Pelasgoi, who, according to tradition, were spread over the northern Aegean and the greater part of the Greek mainland, and were also settled in Crete. Their language survived locally down to the fifth century B.C., and Herodotus describes the people of Attica as Pelasgoi who had changed their language to Greek (Texts 9). The Cyclades and many parts of the Peloponnese were occupied in this period by the Carians, who were also connected with Minoan Crete. Their language must have been known to Herodotus, whose father and uncle bore Carian names; it is known to us only in a few fragments. The Aegean peoples of the second millennium B.C. were also in contact with the Hittites and the Lycians. Thus, it is clear that in this phase of its growth the Greek language was subject to many external changes, which we are unable to trace in detail owing to our ignorance of the other languages.

3. *Phonology.* In PG the IE vowel system was preserved with relatively little change. The tendency to move forward the point of articulation, by which it was subsequently transformed, probably began during the transition from PG to AG. The consonant changes were more extensive, the main factor being a tendency to weaken the force of articulation. Some of the changes given below may belong to AG rather than PG, but for convenience they are given here.

Vowel changes.

(1) IE ə (the so-called 'obscure' vowel, as in Eng. India) became α: πατήρ (Table II A.1).

(2) IE ā became η in Ionic and Attic, except that in Attic it was preserved after ρ, ε or ι: Att. ὥρα ταμίας, Ion. ὥρη ταμίης. In early Ionic the letter H had been used for the intermediate vowel (Eng. drag) marking the transition from one to the other (V.2). Secondary (that is, derivative) ā was affected in some words but not others: Att. Ion. ἔφηνα

< ἔφᾱνα < *ἔφανσα, but πᾶσα < *πάντγα, τάς < τάνς. Att. κόρη δέρη < κόρϜα δέρϜα show that the loss of Ϝ was later than the vowel shift.

(3) IE āi ēi ōi āu ēu ōu were assimilated to ai ei oi au eu ou except in final position: IE *dyēus > Ζεύς, IE *gwōus > βοῦς, dat. sg. ὥραι λόγωι (later written ὥρᾳ λόγῳ).

(4) IE y was reduced initially to a breathing (ἧπαρ =Lat. iecur), with some exceptions (ζυγόν=Lat. iugum) which have not been explained. In other positions it was lost (λόγου < λόγοο < *λογογο < *λογοσγο) or was merged with the preceding vowel: φαίην < *φαγην, μέλαινα < *μελανγα, φαίνω < *φανγω, σφαῖρα < *σφαργα, ἐγείρω < *ἐγεργω, ἄλλο < *αλγο= Lat. aliud.

(5) IE used the nasals m n both as consonants and as vowels; as vowels they are written m̥ n̥. Final -m became -ν (λόγον); m̥ n̥ became α after a consonant (δέκα < *δεκν̥, cf. Lat. decem), α or αν initially (ἄπιστος, ἄναρχος, cf. Lat. in-). Similarly, IE l̥ r̥ (l̥ as in Eng. battle) became αλ λα, αρ ρα: βάλλω πλατύς, καρδία θράσος.

Consonant changes.

(6) IE kʷ gʷ gʷh became π τ or κ, β δ or γ, φ θ or χ, according to the nature of the following vowel (κ γ χ when in contact with υ): φέρω = Eng. bear, θυμός =Lat. fumus, θερμός =Lat. formus =Eng. warm, λιμπάνω =Lat. linquo, τι =Lat. quid; λύκος =Lat. lupus, βαρύς =Lat. grauis, γυνή =Eng. queen, ἐλαχύς =Lat. leuis.

(7) IE s- initial was reduced to a breathing before vowels and ρ (ἕξ =Eng. six, ῥέω =Eng. stream) and lost before λ μ ν: νίφα =Eng. snow. Intervocalic -s- was lost: *γενεσος (=Lat. generis) > γένεος > γένους, *ναυτασων (=Lat. nautarum) > ναυτάων > ναυτῶν, *ἐσγην (cf. Lat. essem) > εἴην.

(8) IE -t -d final were lost: *ἔφατ > ἔφη, *ἔφαντ > ἔφαν, *τιδ (Lat. quid) > τι.

(9) IE w was lost in Attic-Ionic: ἴδω < Ϝίδω=Lat. uideo, ῥίζα < *Ϝρίζα =Eng. wort: see XII.3.3.

(10) IE -m final became -ν: see above 5.

(11) IE t usually became σ before ι and Ϝ (assibilation): φᾱτί > φησί, φαντί > φᾱσί, *τϜε > σε, *τϜος > σός.

(12) IE -ky- -kty- -khy- -kʷy- became Ion. -σσ-, Att. -ττ-: *φυλακγω > φυλάσσω, *ἀνακτγα > ἄνασσα, *γλωχγα > γλῶσσα, *pekʷyo (Lat. coquo) > πέσσω, Att. φυλάττω, γλῶττα, πέττω.

(13) IE -ds- -ts- became -σσ- in Aeolic, -σ- in Attic-Ionic: Att. Ion. παισί σώμασι; Aeo. ἐφρόντισσα, Att. Ion. ἐφρόντισα.

Other changes.

(14) Att.-Ion. ηο < āο became εω (quantitative metathesis): Ion. ληός (< λᾱός) λεώς 'people', Att. λεώς; so Att. εᾱ < ηα: ἱερεᾱ < ἱερῆα.

(15) Two successive syllables beginning with an aspirate lost one of the aspirates, usually the first (dissimilation of aspirates): τίθημι (< *θι-θη·μι), ἔχω (< *ἔχω < *σεχω), πέφηνα (< *φέφηνα), λύθητι (< *λυ·θη·θι), ἐτέθην (< *ἐ·θε·θην). Where the second aspirate was lost as a result of consonant combination, the first was retained: ἔχω ἕξω, τρέφω θρέψω (stem θρεφ-); ταχύς 'quick', θάττων (< *θαχχων) 'quicker'. There are, however, many exceptions, due to analogy: φάθι, ἐφάνθην, ἐχέφρων, ἀμφιθαλής. In all these instances the aspirate is protected by the other forms of the word.

(16) IE -ns- (medial) became -ν-, IE -ns (final) became -ς, derivative ns became σ, all with lengthening of the preceding vowel: ἔφηνα < ἔφᾱνα < *εφανσα, λόγους < λόγονς, φᾱσί < φανσί < φαντί.

(17) The loss of intervocalic y, s and w led to the contraction of contiguous vowels. The forms of contraction varied greatly in the different dialects: the Attic forms are given in Table IV C.

(18) Consonant combinations produced by composition or inflection were subject to modification (consonant assimilations): the Attic assimilations are given in Table IV D. The same assimilations were made in speech between words not divided by a pause: τὴμ πόλιν, ἐλ λόγῳ, τὸγ κύριον.

(19) Final -α -ε -ο, and also -ι except in the dat. sg. of the noun and a few other words, were subject to elision, that is, were not pronounced when followed without a pause by a word beginning with a vowel: μετ᾽ αὐτῶν, εἴδετ᾽ αὐτόν, ταῦθ᾽ ὁρῶ (i.e. ταῦθορῶ), ἐφ᾽ ἡμέραν (ἐφημέραν).

4. *Morphology.* The IE system of vowel gradation was already becoming obsolete and was largely obscured by the phonetic changes described above: πάσχω πείσομαι ἔπαθον πέπονθα πένθος πάθος (*πνθσκω *πένθσομαι *ἔπνθον πέπονθα πένθος *πνθος). There were many independent present and aorist stems (φέρω ἔφερον, ἐνέγκω ἤνεγκον). Many presents were formed from aorists by vowel gradation, reduplication, or infixes marking distinctions of aspect: λίπω λείπω λιμπάνω, μένω μίμνω, ἔγνων γιγνώσκω, ἔπαθον πάσχω. Future time was expressed either by the aorist subjunctive, which was perhaps at this stage a present perfective (IX.5), or by a desiderative form in -σ-, which became the normal sign of the future tense. The imperatives, participles and infinitives were increased in number and co-ordinated systematically with the other parts of the verb. In this way the verb was elaborated as a highly flexible instrument capable of expressing with great subtlety ideas of motion and change.

It dominated the syntax of the language, and even nouns were drawn into its orbit: πένθος mourning (active), πάθος plight (passive); φρόνησις thought (active), φρόνημα a thought (passive); λῆψις seizure (active), λῆμμα a receipt (passive), λαβή handle (instrumental). The noun, on the other hand, was simplified. Of the eight IE cases (including the vocative) three were discarded, and five retained (VII.4). The discarded cases were those that had expressed concrete relations (separation, location, instrument); those that were retained (except the vocative) expressed abstract, purely grammatical, relations (subject, object, dependence). This development from concrete to abstract in the noun may be compared with the development from aspect (concrete) to tense (abstract) in the verb (VIII.4). Finally, in order to compensate for the restrictions imposed on sentence intonation by the fixed pitch accent (VI.3) a wealth of modal particles was evolved. In many instances such particles cannot be translated into written English: for example, the only difference between τί ἐστί; and τί δή ἐστι; is that the second form of the question is more animated than the first.

5. *Syntax.* It is not yet possible to treat Greek syntax systematically from a historical point of view. We should probably assign to this period the creation of the infinitive; the development of tense; the creation of conjunctions and of the secondary uses of the subjunctive and optative; the distinction between the two negative particles οὐ μή (X.4).

6. *Lexicology.* It has been estimated that at least 40 per cent of the AG vocabulary is non-IE in origin. The following examples are selected for their social and historical significance: οἶνος 'wine', ἔλαιον 'olive-oil', σίμβλος 'beehive', κηρός 'wax', πλίνθος 'brick', σωλήν 'drain-pipe', χαλκός 'copper', κασσίτερος 'tin', μόλυβδος 'lead', χρυσός 'gold', σίδηρος 'iron', σάκος 'shield', ξίφος 'sword', θάλασσα 'sea', νῆσος 'island', κυβερνάω 'steer', κάλως 'cable', σάκκος 'sack', κάπηλος 'tradesman', βασιλεύς 'king', ἄναξ 'prince', βωμός 'altar', φόρμιγξ 'lyre'.

XII. CLASSICAL GREEK

1. *Sources.* The term CG is used here in a purely historical sense to denote the Greek language as spoken and written from the earliest records written in the Greek alphabet down to 323 B.C. It is known to us partly from literary texts, which have been preserved in copies dating from the Hellenistic and Byzantine periods, and partly from

inscriptions, which consist mainly of official records, the earliest dating from the seventh century B.C. Our acquaintance with the spoken language is necessarily indirect. The nearest approach to it is to be found in Attic comedy and the dialogues of Plato.

2. *The spoken dialects.* Each city-state used its own dialect. There was, therefore, a multiplicity of local dialects, resembling one another more or less closely according to their origin. There were five main dialects: Attic-Ionic, Arcado-Cyprian, Aeolic, Doric, North-western. After the close of the Dorian invasions and the Ionian migrations their distribution was as follows. Attic was spoken in Attica; Ionic in Euboia (West Ionic), the central Aegean (Central Ionic), and Ionia (East Ionic); Arcado-Cyprian in Arcadia and Cyprus; Aeolic in Boiotia and Thessaly (West Aeolic) and Aiolis (East Aeolic); Doric in the south and east of the Peloponnese, the southern Aegean, and the south-west corner of Anatolia; North-western in the north-west of the Peloponnese, the Ionian Islands, and Central Greece. They were subsequently extended by colonisation and modified by mutual intercourse. Doric was introduced by the Dorians, North-western by the Thessaloi and Aitoloi, about 1000 B.C. From what Herodotus says of the Ionian migration it may be inferred that the Ionic dialect assumed the form in which we know it only after that event (Texts 10). Since North-western elements are found in West Aeolic but not in East Aeolic, it may be inferred that the Aeolic migration took place before the intrusion of North-western. Since Arcado-Cyprian elements have been traced in the Doric of all parts, it may be inferred that Doric was superimposed on Arcado-Cyprian; and in view of the close affinity between Arcado-Cyprian and Aeolic it may be inferred that these two dialects were descended from the Greek of the Achaioi. Finally, since Arcado-Cyprian has certain correspondences with Attic-Ionic, we may suppose that in the N.E. of the Peloponnese, and perhaps elsewhere, it had been superimposed on an older dialect from which was descended the later Attic-Ionic.

3. *Attic-Ionic.* The following characteristics are common to Attic and Ionic:

(1) IE ā > η: see XI.3.2; all the other dialects give ā.

(2) PG āo > ηo > εω: XI.3.14.

(3) Ϝ lost in all positions, with or without compensatory lengthening of the preceding vowel: PG ξένϜος, Ion. ξεῖνος, Att. ξένος, Dor. ξῆνος.

(4) A final -ν might be added to the 3 sg. and 3 pl. endings of the verb and the dat. pl. -σι of the noun: ἔλειπε(ν) φησί(ν) φασί(ν) λείπουσι(ν)

παισί(ν), Ion. λόγοισι(ν). The proper function of this -ν was to prevent elision, but it was used or disused indifferently and so contributed to the instability of final -ν in HG.

(5) Infinitive of athematic presents and aorists in -ναι: εἶναι (Arc. ἦναι, Dor. NW. ἦμεν, Aeo. ἔμμεναι).

(6) Aor. ind. act. pl. 3 -σαν (Table IX.21): Att. Ion. ἔφασαν, Ep. ἔφαν.

(7) εἰ 'if' (Arc. εἰ, Dor. NW. Aeo. αἰ).

(8) -σ- for IE -ds- -ts-: XI.3.13.

(9) ἄν conditional (Arc. ἄν, Cyp. Aeo. κε, Dor. NW. κα).

The following characteristics are found in Attic but not in Ionic:

(10) υ pronounced [ü].

(11) dat. pl. -οις -αις (Ion. -οισι, -ῃσι).

(12) -ττ- for -σσ-: Att. θάλαττα, Ion. θάλασσα.

(13) -ρρ- for -ρσ-: Att. θάρρος, Ion. θάρσος.

The following characteristics are found in Ionic but not in Attic:

(14) IE ᾱ > η after ρ, ε, ι: XI.3.2.

(15) Psilosis (deaspiration) in E. Ionic (also in E. Aeolic), hence Ep. ἠέλιος, Att. ἥλιος.

(16) -αται -ατο for -νται -ντο: see Table IX. 28.

(17) κοῦ κῶς ὅκου ὅκως etc. for ποῦ πῶς ὅπου ὅπως.

There are also differences in vowel contraction: the Attic contractions are given in Table IV C.

4. *Literary dialects.* With the growth of a panhellenic culture there took shape out of the spoken dialects a number of literary dialects associated with different literary forms. The oldest of them is the Epic (or Homeric) dialect. It is based on Aeolic and Arcado-Cyprian but has also a deep-seated Ionic element with a superficial admixture of Attic. Its origin is to be placed in the Mycenean age, or even earlier. Although archaic and artificial, the Homeric poems, of which it is the medium, were so familiar to all educated Greeks that it must have had some influence on the spoken language, as it undoubtedly did on the other literary dialects (Texts 13). As the traditional medium for poetry composed in the epic hexameter and the elegiac couplet, it survived into the Byzantine period. Of the lyric poets, many wrote in their local dialects, such as Sappho and Alkaios in Lesbian Aeolic, Korinna in Boeotian, Anakreon in Ionic; but under the influence of the masters of choral lyric attracted to early Sparta (Terpandros, Alkman, Stesichoros) there grew up for this form of lyric a modified Doric, which was employed by the Boeotian Pindar and the Ionians Simonides and Bakchylides; hence the Doric elements in the choral parts of Attic tragedy. Sicilian

Doric was used in the fifth century by Epicharmos for comedy and in the third by Theokritos for pastoral poetry. The literary forms in which Attic came to the fore were drama and rhetoric. In the drama itself there were morphological and lexical distinctions between the Attic of tragedy, which was somewhat archaic, and the Attic of comedy. Down to the end of the fifth century prose was dominated by Ionic (Hekataios, Herakleitos, Herodotos, Hippokrates), and even Thucydides retained certain Ionic forms such as σσ for Attic ττ. Doric too was cultivated as a prose medium by the Pythagoreans of the West. The next writer of importance, apart from the orators, to use the Attic vernacular for prose was Plato. During the fourth century Attic established its supremacy in this field. Arcado-Cyprian and North-western have left no literary remains.

5. *Beginnings of the Koine.*   With the growth of economic and social intercourse there arose within each dialect group a tendency towards unification. From the middle of the fifth century B.C., when the Confederacy of Delos was converted under Perikles into an Athenian empire, with its capital at Athens, the Attic dialect spread rapidly as an official language throughout the Aegean, and it was spoken generally by educated Greeks, though they still used their local dialect among themselves (Texts 11). Among the common people, one of the main centres for the growth of a mixed vernacular was the Peiraieus, the seaport of Athens, inhabited by Greeks from all parts of the Mediterranean. We hear complaints about the 'impurity' of spoken Attic as early as the fifth century B.C. (Texts 12). In this way the conditions were created for the formation of the Hellenistic Koine, which was mainly Attic but included many elements drawn from Ionic and some from the other dialects.

XIII. HELLENISTIC GREEK

1. *Sources.*   Our knowledge of HG is derived from literary texts, inscriptions and papyri. Of the literary texts the most important are those written in the new standard language known as the Hellenistic Koine or simply the Koine. These include the Greek translation of the Old Testament, dating from the III-IInd centuries B.C., and the New Testament (NT). The inscriptions come from all parts of the Greek-speaking world, the papyri almost entirely from Egypt. These are contemporary documents. The papyri, which range from legal contracts to private letters, written by people of all classes and several nationalities,

are specially important, because they give us an insight into the speech of the common people. We have a fuller knowledge of HG, spoken and written, than of any other ancient language.

2. *The expansion of Greek.* Greek had been spoken at the Macedonian court since the fifth century B.C. Alexander the Great studied under Aristotle, an Ionian by birth who had lived for many years at Athens. After Alexander's conquest of the Persian Empire, Attic became, in the form of the Koine, the official language of the Macedonian Empire, which extended as far as the borders of India. Its principal cities were Alexandria, Ephesos, Pergamos, Seleukia and Antioch. The Koine was spoken as a second language (Texts 17). It is uncertain how widely it was known in the countryside, but except in some of the cities it did not replace the native languages. In this respect it differed from Latin, which replaced the native languages of Gaul and Spain. The reason for the difference lies partly in the high level of civilisation which had long prevailed in the Near East, as compared with Western Europe, and partly in the circumstances of the Macedonian conquest, which led, not to plunder of the conquered areas, but to their economic development through the growth of trade. Since its function was to mediate between the new cities springing up in all parts of the Empire and between the different nationalities residing in each city, the Koine was able, despite local variations, to preserve its unity. In Greece itself the old dialects lingered on as patois (Texts 22).

3. *The Koine.* The transition from CG to HG is comparable with the transition from PG to AG. In both periods the language was extended to peoples whose native languages were not Greek. The principal characteristics of the Koine are the following:

(1) Pitch was superseded by stress; the ancient system of vowel quantity disappeared.

(2) The number of vowels was reduced by continuing the AG tendency to move forward the point of articulation (XI.3): αι > ε, ει ιει ειει > ι ο > ω, οι > υ [ü].

(3) In the noun, under the influence of -ν movable (XII.3.4), final-ν came to be used indiscriminately (ἐν ᾿Αλεξανδρείαν) and so produced a new type of accusative (χεῖραν for χεῖρα), marking the first step in the elimination of the athematic noun (see XIV.3.2).

(4) In the verb, the optative disappeared; the infinitive, after becoming commoner than ever in construction with prepositions (as in the NT), gave way to the use of ἵνα with the subjunctive; the perfect (under the influence of Latin) came to be used as a preterite in place of the aorist

and then disappeared; the imperfect and aorist were reorganised on a new uniform basis (III.4); the athematic presents were assimilated to the thematic (CG δεικνύω for δείκνυμι and ὀμνύω for ὄμνυμι were well established in Attic; HG gives ἱστάνω and στήκω for ἵστημι, δίδω for δίδωμι, ῥήσσω for ῥήγνυμι, etc.); the middle voice gave way to the active (Mt 26.51 ἀπέσπασεν τὴν μάχαιραν αὐτοῦ, cf. Mk 14.47 ἀποσπασάμενος τὴν μάχαιραν), retaining only its reflexive and reciprocal functions (MG λούζομαι, γνωρίζονται).

(5) The particle ἄν was replaced by a periphrasis (Test. XII Patr. 1040a εἰ μὴ ὁ Ἰακὼβ ὁ πατὴρ ἡμῶν προσεύξατο περὶ ἐμοῦ, ἤθελε Κύριος ἀνελεῖν με) or lost its force (ParP. 26, II c. BC ὅταν ἔβημεν).

(6) With the loss of the pitch accent, sentence intonation became free, and hence the variable word order, used in CG to mark the emphasis, ceased to be indispensable: Mt 22.32 οὐκ ἔστιν ὁ θεὸς θεὸς νεκρῶν, ἀλλὰ ζώντων (for οὐ τῶν νεκρῶν θεός ἐστιν ὁ θεός, ἀλλὰ τῶν ζώντων). The old modal particles thus became redundant and disappeared.

(7) In lexicology, Attic words inflected anomalously were replaced by the corresponding forms of other dialects or by other words: Att. λεώς HG λαός, Att. νεώς HG ναός, Att. ναῦς HG πλοῖον, Att. ὅς HG χοῖρος, Att. οἶς HG πρόβατον. The elimination of homophones and morphological anomalies created by the phonetic changes described above played an important part in the transition from AG to MG.

In general, these developments may be regarded as a complex series of consecutive changes due to external contacts. Their significance may be measured by the fact that the Koine is closer to the MG vernacular than it is to Homeric Greek.

4. *Atticism.* After the Roman conquest, which brought the economic expansion of the Near East to an end, many writers set themselves the aim of reviving classical Attic as a literary medium in place of the Koine, which they despised as vulgar (Texts 21). This development, known as Atticism, left a permanent mark on the evolution of the language. Hitherto all Greeks had taken a common pride in their language, which, notwithstanding dialect differences, they had regarded as one; but from the first century of our era down to the present day the language has been torn by a conflict between the artifical medium of the governing class and the living speech of the people. In keeping with this conservative tradition, the AG orthography has been preserved without regard to changes in pronunciation.

XIV. BYZANTINE AND MODERN GREEK

1. *The literary language.* For two centuries after the foundation of Constantinople (330 A.D.) the official language was Latin. During the VI-IXth centuries, owing to the collapse of the Western Empire and the separation of the Eastern and Western Churches, Latin was supplanted by Greek, the language of the Church and of the people. The new official language was the Atticistic Greek of the Hellenistic period. The secular literature was written in the same medium, but with varying degrees of Atticism, and in some writers we find forms and usages drawn from the language of the people. Such were Malalas (VI c. A.D.), Leontios (VII c. A.D.) and Konstantinos Porphyrogennetos (X c. A.D.). The spoken language of the earlier centuries survives only in a few scraps of popular songs (Texts 26) and in some papyrus letters (Texts 25). The earliest poems in the MG vernacular date from the twelfth century A.D.

2. *The ecclesiastical language.* The language, like the teaching, of the Church was founded on the scriptures; and the early Fathers had been proud to use NT Greek, which they defended against pagan ridicule by claiming that only the language of the people was a fit medium for divine truth (Texts 23). It was on this basis that the traditional forms of the liturgy took shape. Later ecclesiastical writers conformed to the prevailing Atticist tradition, but NT Greek remained imbedded in the liturgy and so helped to mould the language of the Byzantine hymns, which was archaic but coherent and in general free from pedantry, just as the hymns themselves were free from the lifeless conventions of classical prosody (Texts 24). The place of these hymns in the life of the period may be compared with that of the Homeric poems in classical Greece. Many of them were included in the regular services of the Church, which played an important part in maintaining the Greek language and culture under Turkish rule.

3. *Characteristics of BG and MG.*

A. Phonology: see Table V.

B. Morphology: see Table XVI.

(1) The dative was merged into the genitive: καλὴ μέρα σου.

(2) Athematic nouns in -ηρ -ωρ -ων were reconstructed: πατήρ πατέρα > πατέρας πατέραν, μητέρα μητέραν, so ρήτορας, δαίμονας, also γέρων γέροντα > γέρος γέρον, cf. ἀσχήμων > ἄσκημος. (Similar forms occur sporadically in AG: Cyp. ἰγατειραν=Ep. ἰητῆρα, Ion. φύλακος=φύλαξ.)

(3) Thematic nouns in -ις were assimilated to nouns in -η: πόλις > πόλη (acc. πόλην, gen. πόλης etc., like λύπη).

(4) Many nouns were remodelled on the neuter diminutive -ιον > -ιν > -ι: χέρι (< χέριον), πόδι (< πόδιον), μάτι (< ὀμμάτιον).

(5) The pl. endings -αι -ας became -ες: ὧραι ὧρας > ὧρες.

(6) The adverbial ending -ως was replaced by the neut. pl. -α.

(7) ἡμεῖς ὑμεῖς, having become homophones, were reconstructed as ἐμεῖς ἐσεῖς after ἐμέ ἐσέ (ἐσέ for σέ on the analogy of ἐμέ).

(8) αὐτός became a demonstrative pronoun like οὗτος (> τοῦτος) but preserved its function as third personal pronoun in the forms τόν τήν τό etc. (< ἀτόν ἀτήν ἀτό).

(9) The relative pronoun ὅς ἥ ὅ was replaced in the written language by ὁ ὁποῖος etc. (cf. Ital. il quale), in the spoken language by ὁπού (AG ὅπου, MG πού) indeclinable.

(10) The optative was lost and replaced by periphrastic expressions with θέλω: θέλω νὰ εἶχα (θὰ εἶχα) 'I should have'.

(11) The future was reconstructed on the basis of θέλω ἵνα > θενά > θά with the subjunctive: θὰ γράφω (imperfective), θὰ γράψω (perfective).

(12) The infinitive survived only in the forms γράψειν (MG γράψει from AG γράψειν for γράψαι) active and γραφῆν (MG γραφῆ from AG γραφῆναι) passive, which were constructed with ἔχω to replace the lost perfect.

(13) Two participles remained, γράφοντας (indeclinable) active and ἐγραμμένος (MG γραμμένος, AG γεγραμμένος) passive.

(14) Pre. pl. 3 -ουσι was replaced by -ουν on the analogy of the impf. aor. -αν: γράφουν(ε) ἔγραφαν ἔγραψαν. Conversely, in some dialects, the impf. aor. -αν was replaced by -ασι on the analogy of -ουσι: γράφουσι ἐγράφασι ἐγράψασι.

(15) The imperative third person was replaced by ἄς (AG ἄφες) with the subjunctive.

(16) The aor. mid. was lost and the aor. pas. was reconstructed on the basis of the old perfect active: ἐλύθηκα < ἐλύθην, cf. λέλυκα.

(17) The verb εἰμί was reconstructed as a medio-passive (Table XIII).

(18) The pre. infix -ν- was developed: pre. φέρνω, impf. ἔφερνα, aor. ἔφερα, fut. θὰ φέρνω, θὰ φέρω.

(19) The contracted verbs in -ῶ (-άω) and -ῶ (-έω) were partly merged (see Table XVI E); the contracted verbs in -ῶ (-όω) were reconstructed with the infix -ν-: δηλώνω < δηλῶ (-όω).

(20) The impf. of contracted verbs was formed in -οῦσα (φιλῶ ἐφιλοῦσα) on the analogy of the 3 pl. HG ἐφιλοῦσαν for ἐφίλουν. These changes were effected gradually and irregularly over the period 500-1500 A.D.

C. Lexicology:

(21) Many Latin words were adopted in BG and some of these survive: ἀκουμπῶ accumbo 'lean', κάμαρα camera 'room', πόρτα porta 'door', σπίτι hospitium 'house'. MG has borrowed many words from Turkish, Italian and Albanian (τουφέκι 'rifle', βαπόρι 'steamboat', λουλούδι 'flower') but the vocabulary remains predominantly Greek. The following etymologies may be noted: ἀκόμη < ἀκμήν, γρήγορος < ἐγρηγορώς, ἐδῶ < ὧδε, δικός < εἰδικός, ἔτσι < οὑτωσί, κάθε from καθένας < καθείς based on AG εἷς καθ' ἕνα, κανείς from (οὐ) κἂν εἷς, μπορῶ < εὐπορῶ, ξέρω ἤξερα based on AG ἐξηῦρον, νερό < νεαρόν, πάω πῆγα < ὑπάγω ὑπῆγον, μά < μόνα for μόνον, πιά πιό < πλέον, τέτοιος based on τι τοῖον, τώρα < τῇ ὥρᾳ (cf. Ital. allora).

4. *The language question.* In MG, as in most modern languages, there are clearly-marked differences between the spoken language of the common people, divided as it is into regional and local dialects, and the literary language used in speech and writing by the educated classes (διγλωσσία). But the situation of MG is complicated by a third factor. This is the so-called 'purist' language (ἡ καθαρεύουσα)—an artificial medium elaborated by eighteenth-century writers and adopted after the liberation (1821) as the official medium of the army, law-courts, civil service, schools and universities. The attempt to impose this medium in place of the spoken language (ἡ δημοτική) gave rise to the 'language question' (τὸ γλωσσικὸ ζήτημα), which has been bitterly contested. The καθαρεύουσα is still maintained in official and academic circles (Texts 33), but the language of the people has prevailed both in daily life and in creative literature, prose and verse (Texts 34-36). It is developing a standard form free from local pecularities and drawing for its technical vocabulary on the inexhaustible treasury of Ancient Greek.

XV. TEXTS

(The originals of Nos. 1-7, 18-20, 25 are without breathings or accents.)

CLASSICAL GREEK

Epigraphical

1 Central Ionic (Naxos). VIc. Buck GD no. 6.

Νικανδρη μ' ανεθεκεν hεκηβολοι ιοχεαιρηι,
qορη Δεινοδικηο το Ναξσιο, εξσοχος αλhον,
Δεινομενεος δε κασιγνετη, Φhραξσο δ' αλοχος νυν.

[Attic translation. Νικάνδρα μ' ἀνέθηκεν ἐκηβόλῳ ἰοχεαίρᾳ, κόρη

Δεινοδίκου τοῦ Ναξίου, ἔξοχος ἄλλων, Δεινομένους δὲ κασιγνήτη, Φράξου δ' ἄλοχος νῦν.]

2 Arcado-Cyprian (Mantinea). Vc. Buck no. 17.

Φοφλεασι οἰδε ἰν 'Αλεαν· [proper names]. ὀσεοι ἀν χρεστεριον κακρινε ἐ γνοσιαι κακριθεε τον χρεματον, πε τοις Φοικιαταις τας θεο ἐναι, κα Φοικιας δασασσθαι τας ἀν ὀδ' ἐασας. εἰ τοις Φοφλεκοσι ἐπι τοιδ' ἐδικασ-αμεν, ἀ τε θεος κας οἱ δικασσται, ἀπυσεδομινος τον χρεματον το λαχος, ἀπεχομινος κα τορρεντερον γενος ἐναι ἀματα παντα ἀπυ τοι ἱεροι, ἱλαον ἐναι· εἰ δ' ἀλλα σις ἐατοι κα τοννυ, ἰνμενφες ἐναι.

[Attic translation. 'Ωφλήκασιν οἵδε τῇ 'Αλέᾳ· [proper names]. ὅτῳ ἀν τὸ χρηστήριον κατακρίνῃ ἢ δημοσίᾳ κατακριθῇ τῶν χρημάτων, μετὰ τῶν οἰκετῶν τῆς θεοῦ εἶναι, καὶ οἰκίας δάσασθαι τὰς ἐνθάδε οὔσας. εἰ τοῖς ὠφληκόσιν ἐπὶ τῷδ' ἐδικάσαμεν, ἥ τε θεὸς καὶ οἱ δικασταί, ἀπο-δεδομένους τῶν χρημάτων τὸ λάχος, ἀπεχομένους κατὰ τὸ ἄρρεν γένος εἶναι ἥματα πάντα ἀπὸ τοῦ ἱεροῦ, ἵλεων εἶναι· εἰ δ' ἄλλα τις ἐᾷ κατὰ τῶνδε, ἐμμεμφὲς εἶναι.]

3 Arcado-Cyprian (Cyprus). Vc. [Transcribed from the Cypriot syllabary.] Buck no. 23.

'Οτε ταν πτολιν 'Εδαλιον κατεΦοργον Μαδοι κας ΚετιεΦες ἰν τοι Φιλο-κυπρον Φετει το 'Ονασαγοραυ, βασιλευς Στασικυπρος κας ἀ πτολις 'Εδα-λιεΦες ἀνογον 'Ονασιλον τον 'Ονασικυπρον τον ἰγατεραν κας τος κασιγνετος ἰγασθαι τος ἀνθροπος τος ἰν ται μαχαι ἰκμαμενος ἀνευ μισθον.

[Attic translation. "Οτε τὴν πόλιν 'Ιδάλιον κατεῖργον Μῆδοι καὶ Κητιεῖς ἐν τῷ Φιλοκύπρου ἔτει τοῦ 'Ονησαγόρου, βασιλεὺς Στησίκυπρος καὶ ἡ πόλις τῶν 'Ιδαλιέων ἐκέλευσαν 'Ονήσιλον τὸν 'Ονησικύπρου τὸν ἰατρὸν καὶ τοὺς κασιγνήτους ἰᾶσθαι τοὺς ἀνθρώπους τοὺς ἐν τῇ μάχῃ τετρωμένους ἄνευ μισθοῦ.]

4 West Aeolic (Boeotia). IIIc. Buck no. 44.

Θιος τουχα ἀγαθα. Φαστιαο ἀρχοντος Βοιωτυς, ἐν δε Λεβαδειη Δορκω-νος, Δωιλος 'Ιρανηω ἀντιθειτι τον Φιδιον θεραποντα 'Ανδρικον τυ Δι τυ Βασιλειι κη τυ Τρεφωνιυ ἱαρον εἱμεν, παρμειναντα παρ ταν ματερα 'Αθανο-δωραν Φετια δεκα, καθως ὁ πατειρ ποτεταξε· ἠ δε κα ἐτι δωει 'Αθανοδωρα, εἰσι αὐτη 'Ανδρικος φορον τον ἐν τη θεικη γεγραμμενον· ἠ δε τι κα παθει 'Αθανοδωρα, παρμενι 'Ανδρικος τον περιττον χρονον παρ Δωιλον· ἐπιτα ἱαρος ἐστω μει ποθικων μειθενι μειθεν· μει ἐσσειμεν δε καταδουλιττασθη 'Ανδρικον μειθενι· 'Ανδρικον δε λειτωργιμεν ἐν της θοσιης των θιων οὑτων.

[Attic translation. Θεὸς τύχῃ ἀγαθῇ. Ἀστίου ἄρχοντος Βοιωτοῖς, ἐν δὲ Λεβαδείᾳ Δόρκωνος, Ζώιλος ὁ Εἰρηναίου ἀνατίθησι τὸν ἑαυτοῦ θεράποντα Ἄνδρικον τῷ Διὶ τῷ Βασιλεῖ καὶ τῷ Τροφωνίῳ ἱερὸν εἶναι, παραμείναντα παρὰ τὴν μητέρα Ἀθηνοδώραν ἔτη δέκα, καθὼς ὁ πατὴρ προσέταξεν· ἐὰν δὲ ἔτι ζῇ Ἀθηνοδώρα, ἤσει αὐτῇ Ἄνδρικος φόρον τὸν ἐν τῇ θήκῃ γεγραμμένον· ἐὰν δέ τι πάθῃ Ἀθηνοδώρα, παραμενεῖ Ἄνδρικος τὸν περιττὸν χρόνον παρὰ Ζώιλον· ἔπειτα ἱερὸς ἔστω μὴ προσήκων μηδενὶ μηδέν· μὴ ἐξεῖναι δὲ καταδουλώσασθαι Ἄνδρικον μηδενί· Ἄνδρικον δὲ λειτουργεῖν ἐν ταῖς θυσίαις τῶν θεῶν τούτων.]

---

5 East Aeolic (Mytilene). IVc. Buck no. 26.

Διαλλάκταις δ' ἐλεσθαι τον δαμον ἀνδρας εἰκοσι, δεκα μεν ἐκ των κατελθοντων, δεκα δε ἐκ των ἐν ται πολι προσθε ἐοντων. οὐτοι δε πρωτον μεν φυλασσοντον και ἐπιμελεσθον ὡς μηδεν ἐσσεται διαφορον τοις κατελθοντεσσι και τοις ἐν ται πολι προσθ ἐοντεσσι. πραξοισι δε και περι των ἀμφισβατημενων κτηματων ὡς οἱ τε κατελθοντες και προς τοις ἐν ται πολι ἐοντας και προς ἀλλαλοις μαλιστα μεν διαλυθησονται, αἰ δε μη, ἐσσονται ὡς δικαιοτατοι, και ἐν ταις διαλυσιεσσι, ταις ὁ βασιλευς ἐπεκριννε, και ἐν ται συναλλαγαι ἐμμενεοισι παντες και οἰκησοισι ταμ πολιν και ταγ χωραν ὁμονοεντες προς ἀλλαλοις.

[Attic translation. Διαλλάκτας δ' ἑλέσθαι τὸν δῆμον ἄνδρας εἴκοσι, δέκα μὲν ἐκ τῶν κατελθόντων, δέκα δὲ ἐκ τῶν ἐν τῇ πόλει πρόσθεν ὄντων. οὗτοι δὲ πρῶτον μὲν φυλαττόντων καὶ ἐπιμελέσθων ὡς μηδὲν ἔσται διάφορον τοῖς κατελθοῦσι καὶ τοῖς ἐν τῇ πόλει πρόσθεν οὖσιν. πράξουσι δὲ καὶ περὶ τῶν ἀμφισβητουμένων κτημάτων, ὡς οἵ τε κατελθόντες καὶ πρὸς τοὺς ἐν τῇ πόλει ὄντας καὶ πρὸς ἀλλήλους μάλιστα μὲν διαλυθήσονται, εἰ δὲ μή, ἔσονται ὡς δικαιότατοι, καὶ ἐν ταῖς διαλύσεσιν, ἃς ὁ βασιλεὺς ἐπέκρινε, καὶ ἐν τῇ συναλλαγῇ ἐμμενοῦσι πάντες καὶ οἰκήσουσι τὴν πόλιν καὶ τὴν χώραν ὁμονοοῦντες πρὸς ἀλλήλους.]

---

6 North-western (Olympia). VIc. Buck no. 62.

Ἀ Ϝρατρα τοιρ Ϝαλειοις και τοις Ἐρϝαοιοις. συνμαχια κ' ἐα ἑκατον Ϝετεα, ἀρχοι δε κα τοΐ. αἰ δε τι δεοι αἰτε Ϝεπος αἰτε Ϝαργον, συνεαν κ' ἀλαλοις τα τ' ἀλα και παρ πολεμο. αἰ δε μα συνεαν, ταλαντον κ' ἀργυρο ἀποτινοιαν τοι Δι Ολυνπιοι τοι καδαλεμενοι λατρειομενον. αἰ δε τιρ τα γραφεα ταΐ καδαλεοιτο αἰτε Ϝετας αἰτε τελεστα αἰτε δαμος, ἐν τέπιαροι κ' ἐνεχοιτο τοι 'νταυτ' ἐγραμενοι.

[Attic translation. Ἡ ῥήτρα τοῖς Ἠλείοις καὶ τοῖς Ἡραφοίοις. συμμαχία ἔστω ἑκατὸν ἔτη, ἀρχέτω δὲ τόδε. εἰ δέ τι δέοι εἴτ' ἔπος εἴτ' ἔργον, συνιόντων ἀλλήλοις τά τ' ἄλλα καὶ περὶ πολέμου. εἰ δὲ μὴ σύνειεν,

τάλαντον ἀργύρου ἀποτινέσθων τῷ Διὶ τῷ Ὀλυμπίῳ οἱ καταδηλούμενοι
ἱερούμενον. εἰ δέ τις τὰ γράμματα τάδε καταδηλοῖτο, εἴτ᾽ ἔτης εἴτε τε-
λεστὴς εἴτε δῆμος, ἐν τῷ ἐφιέρῳ ἐνεχέσθω τῷ ἐνταῦθα γεγραμμένῳ.]

7 Doric (Crete). V c. Buck no. 117. vii. Laws of Gortyna.

Ταμ πατροιοκον ὀπυιεθαι ἀδελπιοι το πατρος τον ιοντον τοι πρειγιστοι.
αἰ δε κα πλιες πατροιοκοι ιοντι κἀδελπιοι το πατρος, τοι ἐπιπρειγιστοι ὀπυιεθαι. αἰ δε κα με ιοντι ἀδελπιοι το πατρος, υἱεεδ δε ἐκς ἀδελπιον, ὀπυιέθαι
ιοι τοι ες το πρειγιστο. αἰ δε κα πλιες ιοντι πατροιοκοι κυἱεες ἐκς ἀδελπιον,
ἀλλοι ὀπυιεθαι τοι ἐπι τοι ἐς το πρειγιστο. μιαν δ᾽ ἐκεν πατροιοκον τον
ἐπιβαλλοντα, πλιαδ δε με.

[Attic translation. Τὴν ἐπίκληρον γαμεῖσθαι ἀδελφῶν τοῦ πατρὸς
τῶν ὄντων τῷ πρεσβυτάτῳ. ἐὰν δὲ πλείονες ἐπίκληροι ὦσι καὶ ἀδελφοὶ
τοῦ πατρός, τῷ μετὰ τοῦτον πρεσβυτάτῳ γαμεῖσθαι. ἐὰν δὲ μὴ ὦσιν
ἀδελφοὶ τοῦ πατρός, υἱεῖς δὲ ἐξ ἀδελφῶν, γαμεῖσθαι ἐκείνῳ τῷ ἐκ τοῦ
πρεσβυτάτου. ἐὰν δὲ πλείονες ὦσιν ἐπίκληροι καὶ υἱεῖς ἐξ ἀδελφῶν, ἄλλῳ
γαμεῖσθαι τῷ μετὰ τὸν ἐκ τοῦ πρεσβυτάτου. μίαν δ᾽ ἔχειν ἐπίκληρον τὸν
ἐπιβάλλοντα, πλείονας δὲ μή.]

8 Epic.   *Literary*

Iliad 2.681.

Νῦν δ᾽ αὖ τοὺς ὅσσοι τὸ Πελασγικὸν Ἄργος ἔναιον,
οἵ τ᾽ Ἄλον οἵ τ᾽ Ἀλόπην οἵ τε Τρηχῖν᾽ ἐνέμοντο,
οἵ τ᾽ εἶχον Φθίην ἠδ᾽ Ἑλλάδα καλλιγύναικα,
Μυρμιδόνες δὲ καλεῦντο καὶ Ἕλληνες καὶ Ἀχαιοί,
τῶν αὖ πεντήκοντα νεῶν ἦν ἀρχὸς Ἀχιλλεύς.

Ionic

9 Herodotus 1.57.

Ἥντινα δὲ γλῶσσαν ἵεσαν οἱ Πελασγοί, οὐκ ἔχω ἀτρεκέως εἰπεῖν·
εἰ δὲ χρεόν ἐστι τεκμαιρόμενον λέγειν τοῖσι νῦν ἔτι ἐοῦσι Πελασγῶν
τῶν ὑπὲρ Τυρσηνῶν Κρήστωνα πόλιν οἰκεόντων, οἳ ὅμουροί κοτε ἦσαν
τοῖσι νῦν Δωριεῦσι καλεομένοισι (οἴκεον δὲ τηνικαῦτα γῆν τὴν νῦν Θεσσα-
λιῶτιν καλεομένην), καὶ τῶν Πλακίην τε καὶ Σκυλάκην Πελασγῶν οἰκησάντων ἐν Ἑλλησπόντῳ, οἳ σύνοικοι ἐγένοντο Ἀθηναίοισι, καὶ ὅσα ἄλλα
Πελασγικὰ ἐόντα πολίσματα τὸ οὔνομα μετέβαλε, εἰ τούτοισι τεκμαιρόμενον δεῖ λέγειν, ἦσαν οἱ Πελασγοὶ βάρβαρον γλῶσσαν ἱέντες. Εἰ τοίνυν
ἦν καὶ πᾶν τοιοῦτο τὸ Πελασγικόν, τὸ Ἀττικὸν ἔθνος ἐὸν Πελασγικὸν
ἅμα τῇ μεταβολῇ ἐς Ἕλληνας καὶ τὴν γλῶσσαν μετέμαθε.

[Attic translation. Ἥντινα δὲ γλῶτταν ἵεσαν οἱ Πελασγοί, οὐκ ἔχω ἀκριβῶς εἰπεῖν· εἰ δὲ χρὴ τεκμαιρόμενον λέγειν τοῖς ἔτι καὶ νῦν οὖσι Πελασγῶν τῶν ὑπὲρ Τυρρηνῶν Κρήστωνα πόλιν οἰκούντων, οἳ ὅμοροί ποτε ἦσαν τοῖς νῦν Δωριεῦσι καλουμένοις (ᾤκουν δὲ τηνικαῦτα γῆν τὴν Θετταλιῶτιν καλουμένην), καὶ τῶν Πλακίαν τε καὶ Σκυλάκην Πελασγῶν οἰκησάντων ἐν Ἑλλησπόντῳ, οἳ σύνοικοι ἐγένοντο Ἀθηναίοις, καὶ ὅσα ἄλλα Πελασγικὰ ὄντα πολίσματα τὸ ὄνομα μετέβαλεν, εἰ τούτοις τεκμαιρόμενον δεῖ λέγειν, ἦσαν οἱ Πελασγοὶ βάρβαρον γλῶτταν ἱέντες. Εἰ τοίνυν ἦν καὶ πᾶν τοιοῦτο τὸ Πελασγικόν, τὸ Ἀττικὸν ἔθνος ὂν Πελασγικὸν ἅμα τῇ μεταβολῇ εἰς Ἕλληνας καὶ τὴν γλῶτταν μετέμαθε.]

10 Herodotus 1.146.

Τούτων δὴ εἵνεκα καὶ οἱ Ἴωνες δυώδεκα πόλιας ἐποιήσαντο· ἐπεὶ ὥς γέ τι μᾶλλον οὗτοι Ἴωνές εἰσι τῶν ἄλλων Ἰώνων ἢ κάλλιόν τι γεγόνασι, μωρίη πολλὴ λέγειν, τῶν Ἄβαντες μὲν ἐξ Εὐβοίης εἰσὶ οὐκ ἐλαχίστη μοῖρα, τοῖσι Ἰωνίης μέτα οὐδὲ τοῦ οὐνόματος οὐδέν, Μινύαι δὲ Ὀρχομένιοί σφι ἀναμεμείχαται καὶ Καδμεῖοι καὶ Δρύοπες καὶ Φωκέες ἀποδάσμιοι καὶ Μολοσσοὶ καὶ Ἀρκάδες Πελασγοὶ καὶ Δωριέες Ἐπιδαύριοι, ἄλλα τε ἔθνεα πολλὰ ἀναμεμείχαται· οἱ δὲ αὐτῶν ἀπὸ τοῦ πρυτανηίου τοῦ Ἀθηναίων ὁρμηθέντες καὶ νομίζοντες γενναιότατοι εἶναι Ἰώνων, οὗτοι δὲ οὐ γυναῖκας ἠγάγοντο ἐς τὴν ἀποικίην ἀλλὰ Καείρας ἔσχον, τῶν ἐφόνευσαν τοὺς γονέας.

[Attic translation. Τούτων δὴ ἕνεκα καὶ οἱ Ἴωνες δώδεκα πόλεις ἐποιήσαντο· ἐπεὶ ὥς γέ τι μᾶλλον οὗτοι Ἴωνές εἰσι τῶν ἄλλων Ἰώνων ἢ κάλλιόν τι γεγόνασι, μωρία πολλὴ λέγειν, ὧν Ἄβαντες μὲν ἐξ Εὐβοίας εἰσὶν οὐκ ἐλαχίστη μοῖρα, οἷς Ἰωνίας μέτεστιν οὐδὲ τοῦ ὀνόματος οὐδέν, Μινύαι δὲ Ὀρχομένιοι αὐτοῖς ἀναμεμιγμένοι εἰσὶ καὶ Καδμεῖοι καὶ Δρύοπες καὶ Φωκεῖς ἀποκεχωρισμένοι καὶ Μολοττοὶ καὶ Ἀρκάδες Πελασγοὶ καὶ Δωριεῖς Ἐπιδαύριοι, ἄλλα τε ἔθνη πολλὰ ἀναμέμικται· οἱ δὲ αὐτῶν ἀπὸ τοῦ πρυτανείου τοῦ Ἀθηναίων ὁρμηθέντες καὶ νομίζοντες γενναιότατοι εἶναι Ἰώνων, οὗτοι δὲ οὐ γυναῖκας ἠγάγοντο εἰς τὴν ἀποικίαν ἀλλὰ Καείρας ἔσχον, ὧν ἐφόνευσαν τοὺς γονέας.]

Attic

11 Plato, *Phaedo* 62a.

Ἴσως μέντοι θαυμαστόν σοι φανεῖται, εἰ τοῦτο μόνον τῶν ἄλλων ἁπάντων ἁπλοῦν ἐστίν, καὶ οὐδέποτε τυγχάνει τῷ ἀνθρώπῳ, ὥσπερ καὶ τἆλλα, ἔστιν ὅτε καὶ οἷς βέλτιον ὂν τεθνάναι ἢ ζῆν· οἷς δὲ βέλτιον τεθνάναι, θαυμαστὸν ἴσως σοι φαίνεται, εἰ τούτοις τοῖς ἀνθρώποις μὴ ὅσιον αὐτοὺς ἑαυτοὺς εὖ ποιεῖν, ἀλλὰ ἄλλον δεῖ περιμένειν εὐεργέτην. — Καὶ ὁ Κέβης ἠρέμα ἐπιγελάσας, Ἴττω Ζεύς, ἔφη, τῇ αὑτοῦ φωνῇ εἰπών.

12 [Xenophon] *Atheniensium Respublica* 2.7.

Εἰ δὲ δεῖ καὶ σμικροτέρων μνησθῆναι, διὰ τὴν ἀρχὴν τῆς θαλάττης πρῶτον μὲν τρόπους εὐωχιῶν ἐξεῦρον ἐπιμισγόμενοι ἀλλήλοις, ὡς ὅτι ἐν Σικελίᾳ ἡδὺ ἢ ἐν Ἰταλίᾳ ἢ ἐν Κύπρῳ ἢ ἐν Αἰγύπτῳ ἢ ἐν Λυδίᾳ ἢ ἐν Πόντῳ ἢ ἐν Πελοποννήσῳ ἢ ἄλλοθί που, ταῦτα πάντα εἰς ἓν ἠθροῖσθαι διὰ τὴν ἀρχὴν τῆς θαλάττης· ἔπειτα φωνὴν πᾶσαν ἀκούοντες ἐξελέξαντο τοῦτο μὲν ἐκ τῆς, τοῦτο δ᾽ ἐκ τῆς. Καὶ οἱ μὲν Ἕλληνες ἰδίᾳ μᾶλλον καὶ φωνῇ καὶ διαίτῃ καὶ σχήματι χρῶνται, Ἀθηναῖοι δὲ κεκραμένῃ ἐξ ἁπάντων τῶν Ἑλλήνων καὶ βαρβάρων.

13 Xenophon *Symposium* 3.5.

Καὶ ὃς εἶπεν· Ὁ πατὴρ ὁ ἐπιμελούμενος ὅπως ἀνὴρ ἀγαθὸς γενοίμην ἠνάγκασέ με πάντα τὰ Ὁμήρου ἔπη μαθεῖν· καὶ νῦν δυναίμην ἂν Ἰλιάδα ὅλην καὶ Ὀδύσσειαν ἀπὸ στόματος εἰπεῖν. — Ἐκεῖνο δ᾽, ἔφη ὁ Ἀντισθένης, λέληθέ σε, ὅτι καὶ οἱ ῥαψῳδοὶ πάντες ἐπίστανται ταῦτα τὰ ἔπη; — Καὶ πῶς ἄν, ἔφη, λελήθοι ἀκροώμενόν γε αὐτῶν ὀλίγου ἂν᾽ ἑκάστην ἡμέραν;

Aeolic

14 Sappho 1.

Ποικιλόθρον᾽ ἀθάνατ᾽ Ἀφροδίτα, παῖ Δίος δολόπλοκε, λίσσομαί σε,
μή μ᾽ ἄσαισι μηδ᾽ ὀνίαισι δάμνα, πότνια, θῦμον·
ἀλλὰ τυῖδ᾽ ἔλθ᾽, αἴ ποτα κἀτέρωτα τᾶς ἔμας αὔδας ἀίοισα πήλοι
ἔκλυες, πάτρος δὲ δόμον λίποισα χρύσιον ἦλθες
ἄρμ᾽ ὑπασδεύξαισα· κάλοι δέ σ᾽ ἆγον ὤκεες στροῦθοι περὶ γᾶς μελαίνας
πύκνα δίννεντες πτέρ᾽ ἀπ᾽ ὠράνω αἴθερος διὰ μέσσω,
αἶψα δ᾽ ἐξίκοντο· σὺ δ᾽, ὦ μάκαιρα, μειδιαίσαισ᾽ ἀθανάτῳ προσώπῳ
ἤρε᾽, ὄττι δηὖτε πέπονθα, κὤττι δηὖτε κάλημμι,
κὤττι μοι μάλιστα θέλω γένεσθαι μαινόλᾳ θύμῳ· <Τίνα δηὖτε Πείθω
μαῖσ᾽ ἄγην ἐς σὰν φιλότατα; τίς σ᾽, ὦ Ψάπφ᾽, ἀδικήει;
Καὶ γάρ, αἰ φεύγει, ταχέως διώξει, αἰ δὲ δῶρα μὴ δέκετ᾽, ἀλλὰ δώσει,
αἰ δὲ μὴ φίλει, ταχέως φιλήσει᾽ κωὐκ ἐθέλοισα.>
Ἔλθε μοι καὶ νῦν, χαλέπαν δὲ λῦσον ἐκ μερίμναν, ὄσσα δέ μοι τέλεσσαι
θῦμος ἰμέρρει, τέλεσον, σὺ δ᾽ αὔτα σύμμαχος ἔσσο.

Doric

15 Pindar, *Olympians* 1.

Ἄριστον μὲν ὕδωρ, ὁ δὲ χρυσὸς αἰθόμενον πῦρ
ἅτε διαπρέπει νυκτὶ μεγάνορος ἔξοχα πλούτου·
εἰ δ᾽ ἄεθλα γαρύεν ἔλδεαι, φίλον ἦτορ, μηκέθ᾽ ἁλίου σκόπει
ἄλλο θαλπνότερον ἐν ἁμέρᾳ φαεννὸν ἄστρον ἐρήμας δι᾽ αἰθέρος,

μηδ' 'Ολυμπίας ἀγῶνα φέρτερον αὐδάσομεν·
ὅθεν ὁ πολύφατος ὕμνος ἀμφιβάλλεται
σοφῶν μητίεσσι κελαδεῖν Κρόνου παῖδ' ἐς ἀφνεὰν ἱκομένους
μάκαιραν Ἱέρωνος ἑστίαν,
θεμιστεῖον ὃς ἀμφέπει σκᾶπτον ἐν πολυμάλῳ
Σικελίᾳ, δρέπων μὲν κορυφὰς ἀρετᾶν ἀπὸ πασᾶν,
ἀγλαΐζεται δὲ καὶ μουσικᾶς ἐν ἀώτῳ,
οἷα παίζομεν φίλαν ἄνδρες ἀμφὶ θαμὰ τράπεζαν.

---

16 Theocritus *Idylls* 3.6.

Ὦ χαρίεσσ' 'Αμαρυλλί, τί μ' οὐκέτι τοῦτο κατ' ἄντρον
παρκύπτοισα καλεῖς τὸν ἐρωτύλον; ἦ ῥά με μισεῖς;
ἦ ῥά γέ τοι σιμὸς καταφαίνομαι ἐγγύθεν ἦμεν,
νύμφα, καὶ προγένειος; ἀπάγξασθαί με ποησεῖς.
Ἠνίδε τοι δέκα μῆλα φέρω· τηνῶθε καθεῖλον,
ὧ μ' ἐκέλευ καθελεῖν τύ· καὶ αὔριον ἄλλα τοι οἰσῶ.
θᾶσαι μάν, θυμαλγὲς ἐμὶν ἄχος· αἴθε γενοίμαν
ἁ βομβεῦσα μέλισσα, καὶ ἐς τεὸν ἄντρον ἱκοίμαν,
τὸν κισσὸν διαδὺς καὶ τὰν πτέριν, ᾇ τὺ πυκάσδει.
Νῦν ἔγνων τὸν Ἔρωτα· βαρὺς θεός· ἦ ῥα λεαίνας
μαζὸν ἐθήλαζεν, δρυμῷ τέ μιν ἔτραφε μάτηρ,
ὅς με κατασμύχων καὶ ἐς ὀστίον ἄχρις ἰάπτει.
ὦ τὸ καλὸν ποθορεῦσα, τὸ πᾶν λίθος· ὦ κυάνοφρυ
νύμφα, πρόσπτυξαί με τὸν αἰπόλον, ὥς τυ φιλήσω·
ἔστι καὶ ἐν κενεοῖσι φιλήμασιν ἁδέα τέρψις.

HELLENISTIC GREEK

17 *Acts of the Apostles* 14.7.

Καί τις ἀνὴρ ἐν Λύστροις ἀδύνατος τοῖς ποσὶν ἐκάθητο, χωλὸς ἐκ κοιλίας
μητρὸς αὐτοῦ ὑπάρχων, ὃς οὐδέποτε περιεπεπατήκει. Οὗτος ἤκουε τοῦ
Παύλου λαλοῦντος· ὃς ἀτενίσας αὐτῷ καὶ ἰδὼν ὅτι πίστιν ἔχει τοῦ σωθῆναι,
εἶπε μεγάλῃ τῇ φωνῇ, 'Ανάστηθι ἐπὶ τοὺς πόδας σου ὀρθός. Καὶ ἥλλετο
καὶ περιεπάτει. Οἱ δὲ ὄχλοι, ἰδόντες ὃ ἐποίησεν ὁ Παῦλος, ἐπῆραν τὴν
φωνὴν αὐτῶν Λυκαονιστὶ λέγοντες, Οἱ θεοὶ ὁμοιωθέντες ἀνθρώποις κατέ-
βησαν πρὸς ἡμᾶς· ἐκάλουν δὲ τὸν μὲν Βαρνάβαν Δία, τὸν δὲ Παῦλον
Ἑρμῆν, ἐπειδὴ αὐτὸς ἦν ὁ ἡγούμενος τοῦ λόγου. Ὁ δὲ ἱερεὺς τοῦ Διὸς τοῦ
ὄντος πρὸ τῆς πόλεως αὐτῶν, ταύρους καὶ στέμματα ἐπὶ τοὺς πυλῶνας
ἐνέγκας, σὺν τοῖς ὄχλοις ἤθελε θύειν. 'Ακούσαντες δὲ οἱ ἀπόστολοι Βαρ-
νάβας καὶ Παῦλος, διαρρήξαντες τὰ ἱμάτια αὐτῶν εἰσεπήδησαν εἰς τὸν

ὄχλον, κράζοντες καὶ λέγοντες· Ἄνδρες, τί ταῦτα ποιεῖτε; καὶ ἡμεῖς
ὁμοιοπαθεῖς ἐσμὲν ὑμῖν ἄνθρωποι, εὐαγγελιζόμενοι ὑμᾶς ἀπὸ τούτων τῶν
ματαίων ἐπιστρέφειν ἐπὶ τὸν Θεὸν τὸν ζῶντα, ὃς ἐποίησε τὸν οὐρανὸν καὶ
τὴν γῆν καὶ τὴν θάλασσαν καὶ πάντα τὰ ἐν αὐτοῖς ... Καὶ ταῦτα λέγοντες,
μόλις κατέπαυσαν τοὺς ὄχλους τοῦ μὴ θύειν αὐτοῖς.

18 Papyrus Letter (II c. A.D.). Hesseling 6.

Ἀντῶνις Λόγγος Νειλοῦτι τῇ μητρί πλῖστα χαίρειν. Καὶ διὰ πάντων εὔχομαί σαι ὑγειαίνειν. Τὸ προσκύνημά σου ποιῶ κατ' αἰκάστην ἡμαίραν παρὰ τω
κυρίω Σεράπειδει. Γεινώσκειν σαι θέλω, ὅτι οὐχ ἤλπιζον, ὅτι ἀναβένις εἰς τὴν
μητρόπολιν. Χάρειν τοῦτο οὐδ' ἐγὼ εἰσῆλθα εἰς τὴν πόλιν. Αἰδυσοπούμην
δὲ ἐλθεῖν εἰς Καρανίδαν, ὅτι σαπρῶς παιριπατῶ. Αἴγραψά σοι, ὅτι γυμνός
εἶμαι. Παρακαλῶ σαι, μήτηρ, διαλάγητί μοι. Λοιπόν, οἶδα τίποτ' αἰμαυτω
παρέσχημαι. παιπαίδευμαι, καθ' ὃν δῖ τρόπον. Οἶδα ὅτι ἡμάρτηκα. Ἤκουσα
παρὰ τοῦ Ποστούμου τὸν εὑρόντα σαι ἐν τω Ἀρσαινοείτη, καὶ ἀκαίρως
πάντα σοι διήγηται. Οὐκ οἶδες, ὅτι θέλω πηρὸς γενέσται εἰ γνοῦναι,
ὅπως ἀνθρόπω ἔτι ὀφείλω ὀβολόν; σὺ αὐτὴ ἐλθέ, ... παρακαλῶ σαι.
Νειλοῦτι μητρεὶ ἀπ' Ἀντωνίω Λόγγου υείοῦ.

[Ἀντῶνις < Ἀντώνιος. πεπαίδευμαι, cf. MG παιδεύω 'punish'. γενέσται
< γενέσθαι. γνοῦναι: γνῶναι, cf. γνούς.]

19 Papyrus Letter (II c. A.D.). Triantaphyllidis p. 185.

Ἀπίων Ἐπιμάχω τῶι πατρὶ καὶ κυρίω πλεῖστα χαίρειν. Πρὸ μὲν
πάντων εὔχομαί σε ὑγιαίνειν καὶ διὰ παντὸς ἐρωμένον εὐτυχεῖν μετὰ
τῆς ἀδελφῆς μου καὶ τῆς θυγατρὸς αὐτῆς καὶ τοῦ ἀδελφοῦ μου. Εὐχα-
ριστῶ τῶ κυρίω Σεράπιδι, ὅτι μου κινδυνεύσαντος εἰς θάλασσαν ἔσωσε
εὐθέως. Ὅτε εἰσῆλθον εἰς Μησήνους, ἔλαβα βιάτικον παρὰ Καίσαρος
χρυσοῦς τρεῖς, καὶ καλῶς μοί ἐστιν. Ἐρωτῶ σε οὖν, κύριέ μου πατήρ,
γράψον μοι ἐπιστόλιον, πρῶτον μὲν περὶ τῆς σωτηρίας σου, δεύτερον
περὶ τῆς τῶν ἀδελφῶν μου, τρίτον ἵνα σου προσκυνήσω τὴν χέραν, ὅτι
με ἐπαίδευσας καλῶς, καὶ ἐκ τούτου ἐλπίζω ταχὺ προκόσαι τῶν θεῶν
θελόντων. Ἄσπασαι Καπίτωνα πολλὰ καὶ τοὺς ἀδελφούς μου καὶ Σερη-
νίλλαν καὶ τοὺς φίλους μου. Ἔπεμψά σοι εἰκόνιν μου διὰ Εὐκτήμονος.
Ἔστι δέ μοι ὄνομα Ἀντῶνις Μάξιμος. Ἐρρῶσθαί σε εὔχομαι.

Κεντυρία Ἀθηνονίκη. Εἰς Φιλαδελφίαν Ἐπιμάχω ἀπὸ Ἀπίωνος
υἱοῦ. Ἀπόδος εἰς χώρτην πρίμαν Ἀπαμηνῶν Ἰουλιανοῦ λιβλαρίω ἀπὸ
Ἀπίωνος ὥστε Ἐπιμάχω πατρί.

[ἐρωμένον: ἐρρωμένον. βιάτικον < Lat. viaticum. ἐρωτῶ: CG παραιτῶ.
χέραν < χέρα. προκόσαι: προκόψαι. εἰκόνιν < εἰκόνιον. χώρτην πρίμαν
cohortem primam. λιβλαρίω < λιβραρίω < Lat. librario.]

20   Papyrus Letter (II-III c. A.D.). Hesseling 8.

Θέων Θέωνι τῷ πατρὶ χαίρειν.

Καλῶς ἐποίησες· οὐκ ἀπένηχές με μετ' ἐσοῦ εἰς πόλιν. Ἡ οὐ θέλις ἀπενεκκεῖν μετ' ἐσοῦ εἰς Ἀλεξάνδριαν, οὐ μὴ γράψω σε ἐπιστολὴν οὔτε λαλῶ σε οὔτε ὑιγένω σε εἶτα. Ἄν δὲ ἔλθῃς εἰς Ἀλεξάνδριαν, οὐ μὴ λάβω χεῖραν παρὰ σοῦ οὔτε πάλι χαίρω σε λυπόν. Ἄμ μὴ θέλῃς ἀπενέκαι με, ταῦτα γείνετε. Καὶ ἡ μήτηρ μου εἶπε Ἀρχελάῳ, ὅτι ἀναστατοῖ με· ἄρρον αὐτόν. Καλῶς δὲ ἐποίησες· δῶρα μοι ἔπεμψες μεγάλα, ἀράκια. Πεπλάνηκαν ἡμᾶς ἐκεῖ τῇ ἡμερα ιβ', ὅτι ἔπλευσες. Λυπόν, πέμψον εἴς με, παρακαλῶ σε. Ἄμ μὴ πέμψῃς, οὐ μὴ φάγω, οὐ μὴ πείνω. Ταῦτα. Ἐρῶσθέ σε εὔχομαι. Τῦβι ιη'.

Ἀπόδος Θέωνι ἀπὸ Θεωνᾶτος υἱῷ.

[ἀπήνεχες < ἀπενήνοχας + ἀπήνεγκες. ἐσοῦ for σοῦ after ἐμοῦ, cf. MG ἐσύ ἐσένα. ἢ οὐ: εἰ μή. ἀπενεκκεῖν: ἀπενεγκεῖν. χαίρω: λέγω χαίρειν. πεπλάνηκαν < πεπλανήκασι + ἐπλάνησαν. ιβ': 12. ὅτι: ὅτε. Τῦβι: the fifth month of the Ptolemaic calendar. Θεωνᾶτος: nom. sg. Θεωνᾶς. υἱῷ: υἱοῦ.]

---

21   Phrynichus, *Eclogae* (II c. A.D.).

Φρύνιχος Κορνηλιανῷ εὖ πράττειν. Τήν τε ἄλλην σου παιδείαν θαυμάζω, ἣν διαφερόντως ὑπὲρ ἅπαντας ὅσοις ἐγὼ ἐνέτυχον πεπαίδευσαι, καὶ δὴ καὶ τοῦτο θαυμαστῶς ἔχω, τὸ περὶ τὴν τῶν καλῶν καὶ δοκίμων ὀνομάτων κρίσιν. Ταῦτ' ἄρα κελεύσαντος σοῦ τὰς ἀδοκίμους τῶν φωνῶν ἀθροισθῆναι, πάσας μὲν οὐχ οἷός τε ἐγενόμην τανῦν περιλαβεῖν, τὰς δὲ ἐπιπολαζούσας, μάλιστα καὶ τὴν ἀρχαίαν διάλεξιν ταραττούσας καὶ πολλὴν αἰσχύνην ἐμβαλλούσας. Οὐ λανθάνει δέ σε, ὥσπερ οὐδ' ἄλλο τι τῶν κατὰ παιδείαν, ὥς τινες ἀποπεπτωκότες τῆς ἀρχαίας φωνῆς, καὶ ἐπὶ τὴν ἀμαθίαν καταφεύγοντες πορίζουσι μάρτυράς τινας τοῦ προειρῆσθαι ὑπὸ τῶν ἀρχαίων τάσδε τὰς φωνάς· ἡμεῖς δὲ οὐ πρὸς τὰ διημαρτημένα ἀφορῶμεν, ἀλλὰ πρὸς τὰ δοκιμώτατα τῶν ἀρχαίων. Καὶ γὰρ αὐτοῖς εἴ τις αἵρεσιν προθείη, ποτέρως ἂν ἐθέλοιεν διαλέγεσθαι ἀρχαίως καὶ ἀκριβῶς ἢ νεοχμῶς καὶ ἀμελῶς, δέξαιντ' ἂν ἀντὶ παντὸς ἡμῖν σύμψηφοι γενόμενοι τῆς ἀμείνονος γενέσθαι μοίρας· οὐ γάρ τις οὕτως ἄθλιος, ὡς τὸ αἰσχρὸν τοῦ καλοῦ προτιθέναι. Ἔρρωσο.

11. Εὐχαριστεῖν οὐδεὶς τῶν δοκίμων εἶπεν, ἀλλὰ χάριν εἰδέναι.

95. Γρηγορῶ, γρηγορεῖ οὐ δεῖ ἀλλὰ ἐγρήγορα λέγειν καὶ ἐγρήγορεν.

100. Ἀκμὴν ἀντὶ τοῦ ἔτι· Ξενοφῶντα λέγουσιν ἅπαξ αὐτῷ κεχρῆσθαι· σὺ δὲ φυλάττου, λέγε δὲ ἔτι.

130. Ἤμην, εἰ καὶ εὑρίσκεται παρὰ τοῖς ἀρχαίοις, οὐκ ἐρεῖς ἀλλὰ ἦν ἐγώ.

333. Βουνός· ὀθνεία ἡ φωνὴ τῆς Ἀττικῆς ... ἐν δὲ τῇ Συρακουσίᾳ ποιήσει καθωμίληται, ἀλλ' οὐ προσίεται ὁ Ἀθηναῖος τὴν ἀλλοδαπὴν λέξιν.

342. Ἐκλείψας ἀδόκιμον, ἀλλὰ τὸ ἐκλιπών.

22 Dio Chrysostomus, *Oratio* I. 60R. (II c. A.D.).

Καὶ δὴ βαδίζων ὡς ἀφ' Ἡραίας εἰς Πῖσαν παρὰ τὸν Ἀλφειόν, μέχρι μέν τινος ἐπετύγχανον τῆς ὁδοῦ, μεταξὺ δὲ εἰς ὕλην τινὰ καὶ δυσχωρίαν ἐμπεσὼν καὶ πλείους ἀτραποὺς ἐπὶ βουκόλι' ἄττα καὶ ποίμνας φερούσας, οὐδενὶ συναντῶν οὐδὲ δυνάμενος ἐρέσθαι, διαμαρτάνω τε καὶ ἐπλανώμην μεσημβρίᾳ σταθερᾷ. Ἰδὼν οὖν ἐπὶ ὑψηλῷ τινὶ δρυῶν συστροφὴν οἷον ἄλσος, ᾠχόμην ὡς ἀποψόμενος ἐντεῦθεν ὁδόν τινα ἢ οἰκίαν. Καταλαμβάνω οὖν λίθους τέ τινας εἰκῇ συγκειμένους καὶ δέρματα ἱερείων κρεμάμενα καὶ ῥόπαλα καὶ βακτηρίας, νομέων τινῶν ἀναθήματα, ὡς ἐφαίνετο, ὀλίγον δὲ ἀπωτέρω καθημένην γυναῖκα ἰσχυρὰν καὶ μεγάλην, τῇ δὲ ἡλικίᾳ πρεσβυτέραν, τὰ μὲν ἄλλα ἄγροικον στολὴν ἔχουσαν, πλοκάμους δέ τινας πολιοὺς καθεῖτο. Ταύτην ἕκαστα ἀνηρώτων· ἡ δὲ πάνυ πράως καὶ φιλοφρόνως δωρίζουσα τῇ φωνῇ τόν τε τόπον ἔφραζεν ὡς Ἡρακλέους ἱερὸς εἴη, καὶ περὶ αὑτῆς ὅτι παῖδα ἔχοι ποιμένα καὶ πολλάκις αὐτὴ νέμοι τὰ πρόβατα· ἔχειν δὲ μαντικὴν ἐκ μητρὸς θεῶν δεδομένην, χρῆσθαι δὲ αὐτῇ τούς τε νομέας πάντας τοὺς πλησίον καὶ τοὺς γεωργοὺς ὑπὲρ καρπῶν καὶ βοσκημάτων γενέσεως καὶ σωτηρίας.

BYZANTINE GREEK

23 Isidorus *ad Petrum*, Migne 78. 1500. (V c.).

Διὸ καὶ τὴν Θείαν αἰτιῶνται Γραφήν, μὴ τῷ περιττῷ καὶ κεκαλλωπισμένῳ χρωμένην λόγῳ, ἀλλὰ τῷ ταπεινῷ καὶ πεζῷ· ἀλλ' ἡμεῖς μὲν αὐτοῖς ἀντεγκαλῶμεν τῆς φιλαυτίας, ὅτι δόξης ὀρεχθέντες, τῶν ἄλλων ἥκιστα ἐφρόντισαν· τὴν δὲ Θείαν ὄντως Γραφὴν ἀπαλλάττωμεν τῶν ἐγκλημάτων, λέγοντες ὅτι οὐ τῆς οἰκείας δόξης, τῆς δὲ τῶν ἀκουσόντων σωτηρίας ἐφρόντισεν. Εἰ δὲ ὑψηλῆς φράσεως ἐρῶεν, μανθανέτωσαν ὅτι ἄμεινον παρ' ἰδιώτου τἀληθὲς ἢ παρὰ σοφιστοῦ τὸ ψεῦδος μαθεῖν. Ὁ μὲν γὰρ ἁπλῶς καὶ συντόμως φράζει, ὁ δὲ πολλάκις ἀσαφείᾳ καὶ τὸ τῆς ἀληθείας ἐπικρύπτει κάλλος, καὶ τὸ ψεῦδος τῇ καλλιεπείᾳ κοσμήσας ἐν χρυσίδι τὸ δηλητήριον ἐκέρασεν. Εἰ δὲ ἡ ἀλήθεια τῇ καλλιεπείᾳ συναφθείη, δύναται μὲν τοὺς πεπαιδευμένους ὠφελῆσαι, τοῖς δ' ἄλλοις ἅπασιν ἄχρηστος ἔσται καὶ ἀνωφελής· διὸ καὶ ἡ Γραφὴ τὴν ἀλήθειαν πεζῷ λόγῳ ἡρμήνευσεν, ἵνα καὶ ἰδιῶται καὶ σοφοὶ καὶ παῖδες καὶ γυναῖκες μάθοιεν. ἐκ μὲν γὰρ τούτου οἱ μὲν σοφοὶ οὐδὲν παραβλάπτονται, ἐκ δὲ ἐκείνου τὸ πλέον τῆς οἰκουμένης προσεβλάβη. Ἄν τινων οὖν ἐχρῆν φροντίσαι, μάλιστα μὲν τῶν πλειόνων, ἐπειδὰν δὲ καὶ πάντων ἐφρόντισεν, δείκνυται λαμπρῶς θεία οὖσα καὶ ἐπουράνιος.

24 Romanos, Hymn. (V-VI c.). Cantarella 1.67.

Τὸν δι᾽ ἡμᾶς σταυρωθέντα / δεῦτε πάντες ὑμνήσωμεν·
αὐτὸν γὰρ κατεῖδε Μαρία / ἐπὶ ξύλου καὶ ἔλεγεν·
<εἰ καὶ σταυρὸν ὑπομένεις, / σὺ ὑπάρχεις / ὁ υἱὸς καὶ θεός μου.>
Τὸν ἴδιον ἄρνα / ἡ ἀμνὰς θεωροῦσα   (α΄)
πρὸς σφαγὴν ἑλκόμενον / ἠκολούθει ἡ Μαρία / τρυχομένη
μεθ᾽ ἑτέρων γυναικῶν / ταῦτα βοῶσα·
<ποῦ πορεύῃ, τέκνον; / τίνος χάριν τὸν ταχὺν / δρόμον τελέσεις;
μὴ ἕτερος γάμος / πάλιν ἔστιν ἐν Κανᾷ
κἀκεῖ νυνὶ σπεύσεις ,/ ἵν᾽ ἐξ ὕδατος αὐτοῖς / οἶνον ποιήσῃς;
συνέλθω σοι, τέκνον, / ἢ μείνω σε μᾶλλον;
δός μοι λόγον, Λόγε, / μὴ σιγῶν παρέλθῃς με,
ὁ ἁγνὴν τηρήσας με, / ὁ υἱὸς καὶ θεός μου.
Οὐκ ἤλπιζον, τέκνον, / ἐν τούτοις ἰδεῖν σε   (β΄)
οὐδ᾽ ἐπίστευόν ποτε / ἕως τούτου τοὺς ἀνόμους / ἐκμανῆναι
καὶ ἐκτεῖναι ἐπὶ σὲ / χεῖρας ἀδίκως·
ἔτι γὰρ τὰ βρέφη / τούτων κράζουσί σοι τὸ / <εὐλογημένος>·
ἀκμὴν δὲ βαΐων / πεπλησμένη ἡ ὁδὸς
μηνύει τοῖς πᾶσι / τῶν ἀθέσμων τὰς πρὸς σὲ / πανευφημίας·
καὶ νῦν τίνος χάριν / ἐπράχθη τὸ χεῖρον;
γνῶναι θέλω, οἴμοι, / πῶς τὸ φῶς μου σβέννυται,
πῶς σταυρῷ προσπήγνυται / ὁ υἱὸς καὶ θεός μου.
Ὑπάγεις, ὦ τέκνον, / πρὸς ἄδικον φόνον,   (γ΄)
καὶ οὐδεὶς σοι συναλγεῖ· / οὐ συνέρχεταί σοι Πέτρος / ὁ εἰπών σοι
<<οὐκ ἀρνοῦμαί σε ποτέ, / κἂν ἀποθνήσκω>>·
ἔλιπέ σε Θωμᾶς / ὁ βοήσας <<μετὰ σοῦ / θάνωμεν πάντες>>·
οἱ ἄλλοι δὲ πάλιν, / οἱ οἰκεῖοι καὶ γνωστοὶ
καὶ μέλλοντες κρίνειν / τὰς φυλὰς τοῦ Ἰσραήλ, / ποῦ εἰσὶν ἄρτι;
οὐδεὶς ἐκ τῶν πάντων, / ἀλλ᾽ εἷς ὑπὲρ πάντων,
θνήσκεις, τέκνον, μόνος, / ἀνθ᾽ ὧν πάντας ἔσωσας,
ἀνθ᾽ ὧν πᾶσιν ἤρεσας, / ὁ υἱὸς καὶ θεός μου.>
Τοιαῦτα Μαρίας / ἐκ λύπης βαρείας   (δ΄)
καὶ ἐκ θλίψεως πολλῆς / κραυγαζούσης καὶ κλαιούσης, / ἀπεκρίθη
πρὸς αὐτὴν ὁ ἐξ αὐτῆς / οὕτως βοήσας·
<τί δακρύεις, μήτηρ; / τί ταῖς ἄλλαις γυναιξὶ / συναποφέρῃ;
μὴ πάθω; μὴ θάνω; / πῶς οὖν σώσω τὸν Ἀδάμ;
μὴ τάφον οἰκήσω; / πῶς ἑλκύσω πρὸς ζωὴν / τοὺς ἐν τῷ ᾅδῃ;
καὶ μὴν, καθὼς οἶδας, / ἀδίκως σταυροῦμαι·
τί οὖν κλαίεις, μήτηρ; / μᾶλλον οὕτω κραύγασον
ὅτι θέλων ἔπαθον, / ὁ υἱὸς καὶ θεός σου.

'Απόθου, ὦ μῆτερ, / ἀπόθου τὴν λύπην·   (ε')

   οὐ γὰρ πρέπει σοι θρηνεῖν, / ὅτι κεχαριτωμένη / ὠνομάσθης·

   τὴν οὖν κλῆσιν / τῷ κλαυθμῷ μὴ συγκαλύψῃς·

   μὴ ταῖς ἀσυνέτοις / ὁμοιώσῃς ἑαυτήν, / πάνσοφε κόρη·

   ἐν μέσῳ ὑπάρχεις / τοῦ νυμφῶνος τοῦ ἐμοῦ.

   μὴ οὖν ὥσπερ ἔξω / ἱσταμένη τὴν ψυχὴν '/ καταμαράνῃς.

   τοὺς ἐν τῷ νυμφῶνι / ὡς δούλους σου φώνει·

   πᾶς γὰρ τρέχων δρόμῳ / ὑπακούσει σου, σεμνή,

   ὅταν εἴπῃς, <<ποῦ ἔστιν / ὁ υἱὸς καὶ θεός μου;>> > . . .

Υἱὲ τῆς παρθένου, / θεὲ τῆς παρθένου

   καὶ τοῦ κόσμου ποιητά, / σὸν τὸ πάθος, σὸν τὸ βάθος / τῆς σοφίας.

   Σὺ ἐπίστασαι ὃ ἧς / καὶ ὃ ἐγένου.   (ιζ')

   Σὺ παθεῖν θελήσας / κατηξίωσας ἐλθεῖν / ἄνθρωπον σῶσαι·

   σὺ τὰς ἁμαρτίας / ἡμῶν ἦρας ὡς ἀμνός·

   σὺ ταύτας νεκρώσας / τῇ σφαγῇ σου, ὁ σωτήρ, / ἔσωσας πάντας.

   Σὺ εἶ θνήσκων, σῴζων· / σὺ παρέσχες τῇ σεμνῇ

   παρρησίαν κράζειν σοι· / ὁ υἱὸς καὶ θεός μου.

   [τὸν ἴδιον 'her own', cf. Texts 4. ἀνθ' ὧν 'because'.]

---

25 Papyrus Letter (VI c.). Ox. Pap. 1874. Hesseling 15.

   Ὁμοίος ἄμμα Εὕα, ὁμοίος Μαρία, καὶ ζῆ Θεός, δέσποτά μου, οὔτε
δίκιε οὔτε ἐμαρτωλὲ οὐτέποτε ἔπαθαν τὸ ἔπαθες· ὅμος δὲν ἐ ἁμαρτίε ὑμῶν
εἰσίν. Ἀλλὰ δοξάζωμεν τὸν Θεὸν ὅτι αὐτὸς ἔδωσεν καὶ αὐτὸς ἔλαβεν·
ἀλλὰ εὔξε ἕνα ὁ Κύριος ἐναπαύσι αὐτοῖς καὶ καταξιώσι ὑμᾶς ἐδῖν ἐν αὐτοῖς
τὸν παράδισον, ὅτι κρίνοντε ἐ ψυχὲ τὸν ἀνθρώπων· αὐτοὶ γὰρ ἀπέρθαν
εἰς κώρφον τοῦ Ἀβραὰμ καὶ τοῦ Ἰσαὰκ καὶ τοῦ Ἰακώβ. Ἀλλὰ παρακαλῶ
σε, κύριέ μου, μὲ βάλης λύπην εἰς τὸ ψυχί σου καὶ ἀπολήσεις τὰ πράγματά
σου, ἀλλὰ εὔξε ἕνα ὁ Κύριος ἀποστίλη ἐπὶ σαὶ τὶν εὐλωγίαν αὐτοῦ.

   [δίκιε: δίκαιοι. ἐμαρτωλέ: ἁμαρτωλοί. δέν < οὐδέν. ἕνα: ἵνα. ἐναπαύσι:
ἀναπαύσῃ. ἐδῖν: ἰδεῖν. ὅτι: ὅτε. ἀπέρθαν: ἀπῆλθον. κώρφον < κόλπον.
μέ: μή. ψυχί < ψυχίον.]

---

26 Anna Comnena 1. 98. [On February 13, 1081, the Emperor Alexius
   Comnenus foiled a conspiracy against him by escaping from Constantinople and joining the army outside the city.]

   Ἔνθεν τοι καὶ τὸ πλῆθος ἀποδεξάμενον τῆς ὁρμῆς τὸν Ἀλέξιον καὶ τῆς
ἀγχινοίας, ἐξ αὐτῶν τῶν πραγμάτων ᾀσμάτιον αὐτῷ ἀνεπλέξαντο, ἐξ
ἰδιώτιδος μὲν συγκείμενον γλώττης, αὐτὴν δὲ τὴν τοῦ πράγματος ἐπίνοιαν
ἐμμελέστατα ἀνακρουόμενον καὶ παρεμφαῖνον τήν τε προαίσθησιν τῆς κατ'
ἐκείνου ἐπιβουλῆς καὶ τὰ παρ' αὐτοῦ μεμηχανημένα. Τὸ δὲ ᾀσμάτιον αὐταῖς
λέξεσιν εἶχεν οὕτως·

Τὸ Σάββατον τῆς Τυρινῆς
Χαρῆς, ᾿Αλέξιε, ἐνόησές το·
Καὶ τὴν Δευτέραν τὸ πρωΐ
῞Υπα καλῶς, γεράκι μου.

Εἶχε δὲ ὧδέ πως ἔννοιαν τὸ διαφημιζόμενον ἐκεῖνο ᾀσμάτιον, ὡς ἄρα, κατὰ μὲν τὸ Τυρώνιον Σάββατον, ᾿Αλέξιε, ὑπέρευγέ σοι τῆς ἀγχινοίας· τὴν δὲ μετὰ τὴν Κυριακὴν Δευτέραν ἡμέραν καθάπερ τις ὑψιπετὴς ἱέραξ ἐφίπτασο τῶν ἐπιβουλευόντων βαρβάρων.

[τὸ Σάββατον τῆς Τυρινῆς, sc. ἑβδομάδος, the first Saturday of Lent. πρωΐ 'morning' < πρωΐον. ὕπα < ὕπαγε. γεράκι < ἱεράκιον.]

---

27 Graeco-Latin Conversation Manual (XI c.). Triantaphyllidis p. 195.

- Καλήμερον· ἦλθες; - ῏Ηλθον. - Bona die; venisti? - Veni.
-῎Ελαβες; ἔδωκας αὐτῷ; -῎Εδωκα. - Accepisti? dedisti illi? - Dedi.
-᾿Απηλλάγης. - Μή τινος χρείαν ἔχεις; - Σὲ ὑγιαίνειν. - Caruisti. - Numquid aliud opus habes? - Te valere.

-᾿Εὰν θέλῃς, ἐλθὲ μεθ᾿ ἡμῶν. - Si vis, veni mecum. - Ubi? - Ad amicum nostrum Lucium; visitemus eum. - Quid enim habet? - Aegrotat. - A quando? Intra paucos dies incurrit. - Ubi manet? - Non longe. - Sis ambula. - Haec est, puto, domus ejus, haec est. - Ecce ostiarius. - Interroga illum, si possumus intrare et videre dominum ejus. Et ille dixit: Quem quaeritis? - Dominum tuum; de salute ejus venimus. - Ascendite. - Quot scalas? - Duas. Ad dexteram pulsate, si tamen venit; processerat enim. - Pulsemus. - Vide, quis est? - Avete omnes. - Dominum tuum volumus visitare; si vigilat, nuntia me. Et ille dixit: Non est hic. - Quid narras? sed ubi est? - Illuc descendit ad laurentum deambulare. - Gratulamur illi; cum venerit, dicas illi nos ad ipsum gratulantes
- Ποῦ; - Πρὸς φίλον ἡμέτερον Λούκιον· ἐπισκεψώμεθα αὐτόν. - Τί γὰρ ἔχει; ᾿Αρρωστεῖ. - ᾿Απὸ πότε; - Πρὸ ὀλίγων ἡμερῶν ἐνέπεσεν. Ποῦ μένει; - Οὐ μακράν. - Εἰ θέλεις, περιπάτει. - Αὕτη ἐστί, νομίζω, ἡ οἰκία αὐτοῦ, αὕτη ἐστίν. -᾿Ιδοὺ ὁ θυρωρός. - ᾿Ερώτησον αὐτόν, εἰ δυνάμεθα εἰσελθεῖν καὶ ἰδεῖν τὸν κύριον αὐτοῦ. Καὶ ἐκεῖνος εἶπεν· Τίνα ζητεῖτε; - Τὸν δεσπότην σου· περὶ τῆς ὑγιείας αὐτοῦ ἐληλύθαμεν. -᾿Ανάβατε. - Πόσας κλίμακας; Δύο· ᾿ς τὰ δεξιὰ κρούσατε, εἰ μέντοιγε ἦλθεν· προελήλυθε γάρ. - Κρούσωμεν. - Βλέπε, τίς ἐστίν; - Χαίρετε πάντες. - Τὸν κύριόν σου θέλομεν ἐπισκέψασθαι· εἰ γρηγορεῖ, μήνυσόν με. Κάκεῖνος εἶπεν· Οὐκ ἔστιν ὧδε. - Τί λαλεῖς; ἀλλὰ ποῦ ἐστίν; -᾿Εκεῖ κατέβη ᾿ς τὸν δαφνῶνα διακινῆσαι. - Συγχαιρόμεθα αὐτῷ· ὅταν ἔλθῃ, εἴποις αὐ-

τῷ ἡμᾶς πρὸς αὐτὸν χαιρομένους   venisse ad salutem ejus, quia
ἐληλυθέναι περὶ τῆς σωτηρίας αὐτοῦ   omnia recte habent. - Sic fa-
ὅτι πάντα ὀρθῶς ἔχει. - Οὕτω ποιῶ.   ciam.

[ὧδε > MG ἐδῶ 'here', cf Texts 2 τας ἀν ὀδ' ἔασας.]

---

28 Anonymus. *Byzantion* 22 (1952). 379. [This note was written in Crete shortly after the fall of Constantinople in 1453.]

Ἔτει ͵αυνγ', 'Ιουνίου κθ' ἡμέρα ἕκτη, ἦλθον ἀπὸ τὴν Κωνσταντινούπολιν καράβια τρία Κρητικά, τοῦ Σγούρου, τοῦ Ὑαληνᾶ, καὶ
τοῦ Φιλομάτου· λέγοντες ὅτι εἰς τὴν κθ' τοῦ Μαΐου μηνός, τῆς ἁγίας
Θεοδοσίας ἡμέρα τρίτη, ὥρα γ' τῆς ἡμέρας, ἐσέβησαν οἱ Ἀγαρηνοὶ εἰς
τὴν Κωνσταντινούπολιν, τὸ φωσάτον τοῦ Τούρκου Τζαλαπῆ Μεεμέτ,
καὶ εἶπον ὅτι ἀπέκτειναν τὸν βασιλέα τὸν κυρ Κωνσταντῖνον Δράγασιν καὶ
Παλαιολόγον. Καὶ ἐγένετο οὖν μεγάλη θλῖψις καὶ πολλὶς κλαυθμὸς εἰς τὴν
Κρήτην διὰ τὸ θληβερὸν μήνυμα ὅπερ ἦλθε, ὅτι χεῖρον τούτου οὐ γέγονεν
οὔτε γεννήσεται. Καὶ Κύριος ὁ Θεὸς ἐλεήσαι ἡμᾶς, καὶ λυτρώσεται ἡμᾶς
τῆς φοβερᾶς αὐτοῦ ἀπειλῆς.

[͵αυνγ': 1453. κθ': 29. καράβι 'ship' < καράβιον < HG κάραβος
'coracle'. φωσάτον: φοσσάτον 'army' < Lat. fossatum. κυρ < κύριον.]

MODERN GREEK

29 Assisae. Laws of Cyprus under the House of Lusignan. (XIV c.). Valetas 1.3.

Ἐλευθερίαν ἡμπορεῖ νὰ δώσει ὁ ἀφέντης ἢ ἡ κυρὰ τοῦ σκλάβου του
εἰς πολλὲς λογές. Ἐὰν ὁ ἀφέντης ἢ ἡ κυρὰ πεῖ ὀμπρὸς τρεῖς μάρτυρες ἢ
ὀμπρὸς δύο, < Ἐγὼ δίδω σου ἐλευθερίαν διὰ τὸν Θεὸν καὶ συντάσσομαί
σου ἀπάρτι νὰ εἶσαι ἀποβγαλμένος>, τὸ δίκαιον κελεύει ὅτι μετὰ τοῦτο
εἶναι κρατημένος νὰ τὸν ἐλευθερώσει. Καὶ ἐὰν ὁ ἀφέντης ἢ ἡ κυρὰ ποίσουν χαρτὶν τῆς ἐλευθερίας, ἐκεῖνον ἀξιάζει· καὶ ἔνι κρατημένος νὰ τὸν
ἐλευθερώσει, ἀκόμη ἂν ἔνι ὅτι νὰ ἦτον ἔξω τῆς χώρας, ὅταν ἐποῖκεν ἐκεῖνον
τὸ χαρτὶν τῆς ἐλευθερίας. Καὶ ἐλευθερίαν ἡμπορεῖ κανεὶς νὰ ποιήσει ἀπὸ
θανάτου του ἢ εἰς τὴν διαθήκην του ἢ ἄνευ διαθήκης, καὶ ἐντέχεται νὰ
ἔνι στερεωμένη, μόνο νὰ ἔχει δύο μάρτυρας ἢ τρεῖς.

[ἡμπορῶ < μπορῶ 'be able' < AG εὐπορῶ. ἀφέντης 'master' < AG
αὐθέντης. κυρά < κυριά < κυρία. λογή 'sort', cf. AG λέγω 'choose',
λογάς 'chosen'. πεῖ < εἴπη. ὀμπρός < ἐμπρός: AG ἔμπροσθε. δίδω <
CG δίδωμι. διά > MG γιά. ἀπάρτι cf. Texts 24.γ.6 ἄρτι: CG νῦν, MG
τώρα. ἀποβγαλμένος 'dismissed': MG βγάλλω < AG ἐκβάλλω. κρατη-

μένος 'obliged'. ποίσουν < ποιήσουν < ποιήσωσι. ἀξιάζει: ἀξίζει. ἀκόμη <
AG ἀκμήν: Texts 21. ἀκόμη ἂν ἔνι ὅτι νὰ ἦτον 'even though (it is
that) he may have been'. ἐποῖκεν < ἐποίησεν + πεποίηκεν: cf. Texts
20 πεπλάνηκαν. κανείς: Chap. XIV.3.22. ἐντέχεται: ἐνδέχεται.]

---

30 Ballad. The capture of Constantinople. Politis p. 12.

    Σημαίνει ὁ Θιός, σημαίνει ἡ γῆς, σημαίνουν τὰ ἐπουράνια,
    Σημαίνει κ' ἡ ἁγιὰ Σοφιά, τὸ μέγα μοναστήρι,
    Μὲ τετρακόσια σήμαντρα κ' ἐξήντα δυό καμπάνες,
    Κάθε καμπάνα καὶ παπᾶς, κάθε παπᾶς καὶ διάκος.
    Ψάλλει ζερβὰ ὁ βασιλιάς, δεξιὰ ὁ πατριάρχης,
    Κι' ἀπ' τὴν πολλὴ τὴν ψαλμουδιὰ ἐσείονταν οἱ κολόνες.
    Νὰ μποῦνε στὸ χερουβικὸ καὶ νά 'βγει ὁ βασιλέας,
    Φωνὴ τοὺς ἦρθε ἐξ οὐρανοῦ κι' ἀπ' ἀρχαγγέλου στόμα·
    <Πάψετε τὸ χερουβικὸ κι' ἂς χαμηλώσουν τάγια·
    Παπάδες, πάρτε τὰ γιερά, κ' ἐσεῖς, κεριά, σβηστῆτε,
    Γιατὶ εἶναι θέλημα Θεοῦ, ἡ Πόλη νὰ τουρκέψει.
    Μόν' στεῖλτε λόγο στὴ Φραγκιά, νά 'ρθουνε τριὰ καράβια,
    Τό 'να νὰ πάρει τὸ Σταυρό, καὶ τἄλλο τὸ βαγγέλιο,
    Τὸ τρίτο, τὸ καλύτερο, τὴν ἁγία τράπεζά μας,
    Μὴ μᾶς τὴν πάρουν τὰ σκυλιὰ καὶ μᾶς τὴ μαγαρίσουν.>
    Ἡ Δέσποινα ταράχτηκε, καὶ δάκρυσαν οἱ εἰκόνες.
    Σώπασε, κύρα Δέσποινα, καὶ μὴ πολυδακρύζεις·
    Πάλι μὲ χρόνους, μὲ καιρούς, πάλι δικά σας εἶναι.

[γῆς: γῆ, cf. πόλις πόλη. ἐξῆντα < ἐξήκοντα. καμπάνα < Lat.
campana. διᾶκος < BG διάκων < AG διάκονος. ζερβός 'left'. κολόνα <
Ital. colonna. μπαίνω μπῆκα μπῶ < AG ἐμβαίνω ἐμβέβηκα ἐμβῶ.
βγαίνω βγῆκα βγῶ < AG ἐκβαίνω ἐκβέβηκα ἐκβῶ. πάψετε < παύσατε.
χαμηλώνω 'to lower': AG χαμηλός, χαμαί ' on the ground'. παίρνω
πῆρα πάρω 'take' < AG ἀπαίρω ἀπῆρα ἀπάρω. κερί 'candle' < κηρίον.
σβήνω σβήστηκα σβηστῶ < AG σβέννυμι ἐσβέσθην σβεσθῶ. τουρκεύω
'turn Moslem', cf. AG μηδίζω. στεῖλτε: στείλατε. Φραγκιά 'Western
Europe'. νά'ρθουνε: νὰ ἔρθουν. βαγγέλιο < εὐαγγέλιον. σκυλί < σκυλίον <
AG σκύλος, σκύλαξ. μαγαρίζω 'pollute' < AG *μεγαρίζω? σωπαίνω
ἐσώπασα: AG σιωπῶ (-άω) ἐσιώπησα. χρόνος 'year'. δικός < ἰδικός
'own'.]

---

31 Μοιρολόγια. Politis p. 219.

    (1) Κάτου στὰ Τάρταρα τῆς γῆς, τὰ κρυοπαγωμένα,
    Μοιρολογοῦν οἱ λυγερὲς καὶ κλαῖν τὰ παλληκάρια.

Τάχα νὰ στέκει ὁ οὐρανός, νὰ στέκει ὁ ἀπάνου κόσμος,
Νὰ στέκουν τὰ χοροστασιά, σὰν ποὺ ἤτανε καὶ πάντα,
Νὰ λειτουργιῶνται οἱ ἐκκλησιές, νὰ ψέλνουν οἱ παπᾶδες;

(2) Γιὰ πές μου, τί τοῦ ζήλεψες αὐτοῦ τοῦ κάτου κόσμου;
Αὐτοῦ βιολιὰ δὲν παίζονται, παιγνίδια δὲν βαροῦνε,
αὐτοῦ συδυὸ δὲν κάθονται, συντρεῖς δὲν κουβεντιάζουν,
Εἶναι κ' οἱ νιοὶ ξαρμάτωτοι κ' οἱ νιὲς ξεστολισμένες,
Καὶ τῶν μαννάδων τὰ παιδιὰ σὰ μῆλα ραβδισμένα.

(3) Καλότυχά εἶναι τὰ βουνά, καλότυχοί εἶναι οἱ κάμποι,
Ποὺ Χάρο δὲν ἀκαρτεροῦν, φονιᾶ δὲν περιμένουν,
Μόν' περιμένουν ἄνοιξη, τόμορφο καλοκαίρι,
Νὰ πρασινίσουν τὰ βουνά, νὰ λουλουδοῦν οἱ κάμποι.

[μοιρολογῶ 'lament': μοῖραν λέγω. λυγερή 'lass', lit. 'lithe': AG λύγος 'withy'. παλληκάρι: AG πάλληξ πάλλαξ 'youth'. στέκω < HG στήκω < ἔστηκα. ψέλνω < ψάλνω < AG ψάλλω. γιά πές < εἶα εἶπέ. βαρῶ 'beat', 'resound': AG βαρύνω. κουβέντα 'conversation' < BG κομβέντος < Lat. conventus. νιός < νέος. μάννα < AG μάμμα. ραβδισμένος 'knocked down with sticks' (ῥάβδοι). κάμπος < Lat. campus. Χάρος Χάρον < AG Χάρων Χάρωνα.. ἄνοιξη < ἄνοιξις, cf. Lat. Aprilis. καλοκαίρι: καλὸς καιρός. ὅμορφος < ἔμορφος < AG εὔμορφος.]

32 Λιανοτραγούδια. Politis pp. 167-9, Pernot p. 38.

(1) 'Απ' ὅλα τἄστρα τοὐρανοῦ ἕνα εἶναι ποὺ σοῦ μοιάζει,
Ἕνα ποὺ βγαίνει τὸ πουρνό, ὅταν γλυκοχαράζει.

(2) Κυπαρισσάκι μου ψηλό, ποιὰ βρύση σὲ ποτίζει,
Ποῦ στέκεις πάντα δροσερὸ κι ἀνθεῖς καὶ λουλουδίζεις;

(3) Μὰ σύ εἶσαι μιὰ βασίλισσα, π' ὅλο τὸν κόσμο ὁρίζεις,
Σὰ θέλεις παίρνεις τὴ ζωή, σὰ θέλεις τὴ χαρίζεις.

(4) Ὄντε σ' ἐγέννα ἡ μάννα σου, ὁ ἥλιος ἐκατέβη
Καὶ σοῦ'δωκε τὴν ὀμορφιὰ καὶ πάλι μετανέβη.

(5) Ποιὸς ἥλιος λαμπερώτατος σοῦ'δωκε τὴν ἀνθάδα,
Καὶ ποιὰ μηλιά, γλυκομηλιά, τὴ ροδοκοκκινάδα;

(6) Σὰν τί τὸ θέλει ἡ μάννα σου τὴ νύχτα τὸ λυχνάρι,
Ὁποὺ'χει μέσ' στὸ σπίτι της τ' Αὐγούστου τὸ φεγγάρι;

(7) Δίχως χιόνια χιονίζουμαι, δίχως βροχιὰ βροχιοῦμαι,
Δίχως μαχαίρια σφάζουμαι, ὄντας σὲ συλλογιοῦμαι.

(8) Θάλασσα, ἀπ' ὅλα τὰ νερὰ καὶ τὰ ποτάμια πίνεις,
Καὶ τὰ δικά μου δάκρυα πιέ, πλατύτερη νὰ γίνεις.

(9) Ὁ ὕπνος περιφέρνεται στὴν κλίνη μου ἀπάνω·
Κλειστὰ τὰ μάτ'α, σὲ θωρῶ· ἀνοίγω τα, σὲ χάνω.

(10) Χελιδονάκι νά γενῶ, στήν κλίνη σου νά ἔρθω,
      Νά κτίσω τή φωλίτσα μου εἰς τά προσκέφαλά σου,
      Νά κελαδῶ νά σέ ξυπνῶ, πάντα νά μέ θυμᾶσαι,
      Νά μέ θυμᾶσαι, λυγερή, ὥστε νά ζῆς καί νά 'σαι.

[λιανός 'small': AG λειῶ (-όω) 'to mash' (λειός 'smooth'). τραγούδι < τραγῴδιον. μοιάζει < ὁμοιάζει. πουρνός < πρωινός. χαράζει 'the day breaks': AG χαράσσω 'engrave', 'mark'. ψηλός < ὑψηλός. βρύση < AG βρύσις 'bubbling up'. σά < σάν < ὡς ἄν. ὄντε < ὄτε. λυχνάρι: AG λύχνος. φεγγάρι (AG φέγγος 'light') for AG σελήνη (σέλας 'light') for μήνη. βροχιά < βροχή. ὄντας < ὄταν. νερό < HG νεαρόν. θωρῶ < θεωρῶ. χάνω ἔχασα 'lose': AG χάσκω ἔχασα 'gape after', cf. χατῶ (-έω) χατίζω 'lack'. φωλίτσα 'nest': AG φωλεά. πάντα 'always' sc. χρόνον, cf. AG διά παντός, sc. τοῦ χρόνου. θυμᾶμαι θυμοῦμαι < AG ἐνθυμοῦμαι.]

---

33   G. Mistriotis, Ῥητορικοί λόγοι, 1913, p. 2. Triantaphyllidis p. 512.

Ἡ γλῶσσα τῶν χυδαϊστῶν εἶναι ἄχρηστος καί ἐν τῇ ποιήσει καί ἐν τῷ πεζῷ λόγῳ. Ἐπειδή δέ ἡ ποίησις θηρεύει τό κάλλος, τά ἀκρωτηριάσματα καί αἱ χυδαιότητες καί ὁ βόρβορος τῶν βαρβαρικῶν λέξεων δέν δύνανται νά οἰκοδομήσωσι Παρθενῶνα. Οἱ ποιηταί δέν εἶναι σκώληκες συστρεφόμενοι ἐν τῷ βορβόρῳ, ἀλλά κατά τόν κύκνον τῆς Βοιωτίας ἀετοί τοῦ Διός ἐν τῷ αἰθέρι τοῦ ποιητικοῦ οὐρανοῦ δολιχοδρομοῦντες. Ἐπειδή δέ ἡ δημοτική γλῶσσα εἶναι πτωχοτάτη καί ἀναρμοδία πρός παραγωγήν νέων λέξεων διά συνθέσεως, δέν ἀρκεῖ πρός δήλωσιν τεχνικῶν καί ἐπιστημονικῶν ὅρων. Ἄν ὀλιγωρήσωμεν, καί διά τήν ὀλιγωρίαν ἐπικρατήσωσιν οἱ χυδαϊσταί, ἡ μέν γλῶσσα διασπᾶται εἰς διαλέκτους, ἡ δέ φυλή εἰς κεχωρισμένας ὁμάδας καί τμήματα προκαλοῦντα νέους κατακτητάς, ἡ δ' ἐκκλησία ἀποχωρίζεται τῆς γλώσσης, δι' ἧς κατανοεῖται τό ἱερόν Εὐαγγέλιον καί τά θεῖα τῶν μελῳδῶν ᾄσματα.

---

34   D. Photiadis, Ζωή καί τέχνη, p. 529.

Θά θέλαμε ἀκόμα νά κάνουμε τούτη δῶ τή διευκρίνιση, γιά νά ἀποφύγουμε μιά τυχόν βασική παρεξήγηση. Τά ὅσα εἴπαμε, δέ στέκονται δόγματα, μά μιά μέθοδος ἔρευνας. Κι' οὔτε ἄς νομιστεῖ πώς ἄν γίνηκαν κάπως ἔτσι, ὅπως τά ἀνιστορήσαμε, τά πράματα στόν ἀρχαῖο Ἑλληνικό κόσμο, αὐτά θά ἐπαναληφθοῦν. Τίποτα δέν ἐπαναλαμβάνεται. Ἄν σχηματίζουμε πολλές φορές μιά ἀντίθετη ἀντίληψη, ἡ αἰτία εἶναι πώς μᾶς ξεγελᾶνε τά ἐξωτερικά σχήματα. Τότε σέ τί θά μᾶς βοηθήσει ἡ διαδρομή πού κάναμε; Ἀσφαλῶς ὄχι νά μιμηθοῦμε τό παρελθόν καί νά φτιάσουμε μιά τέχνη ὅμοια μὲ τὴ δική τους. Ὁ ἀκαδημαϊσμός, σὲ ὅλες τὶς ἐκδηλώσεις του, ἔχει τὸ θάνατο μέσα του ὅπως γυρεύει νὰ ἀναστήσει μορφὲς καὶ περιεχόμενο ποὺ ἀνταποκρίνονται σὲ καταστάσεις ὁλότελα διαφορετικὲς ἀπὸ τὶς δικές μας. Ὁ Παρθενώνας, γιὰ νὰ πάρουμε ἕνα χτυπητὸ παράδειγμα, ἦταν καὶ μένει ἀριστούργημα. Ὁ ἀρχιτέχτονας, μὲ τὰ μέσα ποὺ εἶχε στὴ διάθεσή του, ἔδωσε σ' αὐτὸν τὴν ἀνώτατη καλλιτεχνικὴ ἔκφραση τῆς κοσμοθεωρίας τῆς ἐποχῆς του. Σήμερα ὁ ἀρχιτέχτονας ἔχοντας στὴ διάθεσή του διαφορετικὰ μέσα καὶ διαφορετικὴ κοσμοθεωρία πρέπει νὰ ἀντιμετωπίσει καὶ νὰ βρεῖ διαφορετικὲς λύσεις. Τὸ νὰ ἀντιγράψει ἢ νὰ μιμηθεῖ τὸν Παρθενώνα δὲν ἔχει κανένα νόημα. Εἶναι βέβαιο πὼς ἀπὸ 'να ἀριστούργημα θὰ φτειάξει μιὰ καρικατούρα. Ποτὲ ἂς μὴν ξεχνᾶμε, ὅπως τονίσαμε καὶ στὸν πρόλογο τούτου τοῦ βιβλίου, πὼς τὸ ὡραῖο δὲν εἶναι πάντα τὸ ἴδιο. Ἡ οὐσία του, ποὺ ὅλα ἀλλάζει, πρέπει ἀκατάπαυτα νὰ ἀνακαλύπτεται καὶ νὰ μεταδίνεται ἀπὸ τὸν καλλιτέχνη στοὺς συνανθρώπους του.

[δώ: ἐδῶ. κάπως 'somehow', cf. κάπου κάποτε κάποιος κάμποσος κανείς: Chap. XIV.3.21. κάνω κάμω ἔκανα ἔκαμα 'do', 'make': AG κάμνω ἔκαμον. φτειάνω 'make': AG εὐθύνω. γυρεύω 'seek' < HG γυρεύω 'go round in circles' < γῦρος 'ring', cf. French chercher < Lat. circare. χτυπητός < κτυπητός. μέ < μετά. ξεχνῶ ξέχασα 'forget', cf. χάνω ἔχασα 'lose'.]

35 K. Palamas, Ἴαμβοι καὶ θρῆνοι, p. 39.

Μιὰν αὐγὴ χειμωνιάτικη
Ποὺ φοροῦσε κορώνα
Τὴν καταχνιά, σὰν ὅραμα
Εἶδα τὸν Παρθενώνα.
Μαγικὸ μισοδιάφανο
Τὸν ἔζωνε μαγνάδι
Στὸν ἥλιο ἀγνάντια, κ' ἔλεγεν·
Ἐγὼ εἶμαι τὸ σημάδι
Τοῦ ὡραίου ποὺ δείχνει ἀπόμακρα
Στὴν πλατωσιὰ τοῦ Ἀπείρου
Καὶ τάσπρο στέρεο μάρμαρο
Σὰν τὸν ἀχνὸ τοῦ ὀνείρου.

[κορώνα < Lat. corona. καταχνιά 'mist'. μισοδιάφανο < ἡμισοδιάφανον. ζώνω ἔζωσα < AG ζώννυμι ἔζωσα. μαγνάδι 'cloak'. ἀγνάντια: ἐνάντια. δείχνω ἔδειξα < AG δείκνυμι ἔδειξα. πλατωσιά 'expanse' < πλάτος.]

36 A. Sikelianos, Λυρικὸς βίος, vol. iii, p. 324.

Τὰ χελιδόνια τοῦ θανάτου Σου μηνᾶν μιὰν ἄνοιξη
καινούρια, 'Ελλάδα, κι ἀπ' τὸν τάφο Σου γιγάντεια γέννα.
Μάταια βιγλίζει τῶν Ρωμαίων ἡ κουστωδία τριγύρα Σου.
'Ακόμα λίγο, κι ἀνασταίνεσαι σὲ νέο Εἰκοσιένα!

[μηνῶ < μηνύω: Table XVI.11. καινούριος: AG καινουργῶ (-έω).
βιγλίζω < βίγλα < Lat. vigilia. κουστωδία < Lat. custodia. τριγύρα <
τρίς + γύρω. λίγο < ὀλίγον. ἀνασταίνομαι: AG ἀνίσταμαι.]

XVI. TABLES

KEY TO THE TABLES

1. Hypothetical forms, that is, forms not actually found in written records, are marked with an asterisk.

2. The sign > means 'became' or 'was changed into'; the sign < means 'is derived from'.

3. The tables of the noun and verb are arranged so as to display the underlying connections between the endings. They should be studied in the light of the phonetic laws formulated in XI.3. The following symbols are used:

   (a) The point (·) is used to divide the component elements of a word, e.g. λόγ·ο·ς (stem + theme-vowel + ending);

   (b) The hyphen (-) is placed after that part of the word which is to be repeated when reading off the forms to the right of it, e.g. φύλακ-α -ος -ι (φύλακα φύλακος φύλακι). Where hyphen and point coincide, only the hyphen is used, e.g. φύλακ-α.

   (c) The sign ⌇⌇⌇ means that the form to the left of it is to be repeated in full, e.g. φύλαξ ⌇⌇⌇ (φύλαξ φύλαξ).

   (d) The sign × means that the form preceding it on the left is to be repeated without that part of it which follows the hyphen, e.g. ἰχθύ-ς × (ἰχθύς ἰχθύ), ἔ·δυ-ν -ς × (ἔδυν ἔδυς ἔδυ).

   (e) Where two forms are given in the same box, one above the other, the upper one is the Epic form and the lower is the Attic.

4. The following abbreviations are used:
   IE Indo-European; PG Prehistoric Greek; AG Ancient Greek;

CG Classical Greek; HG Hellenistic Greek; BG Byzantine Greek; MG Modern Greek; Ep. Epic; Ion. Ionic; Att. Attic; Aeo. Aeolic; Dor. Doric; Arc. Arcadian; Cyp. Cyprian; NW. North-western;

Sg. singular; pl. plural; N nom. nominative; V voc. vocative; A acc. accusative; G gen. genitive; D dat. dative; m. masculine; f. feminine; n. neuter; mf. common (masculine or feminine);

Pri. primary; sec. secondary; act. active; mid. middle; pas. passive; mp. medio-passive; ind. indicative; sub. subjunctive; opt. optative; imp. imperative; inf. infinitive; ptc. participle;

pre. present; impf. imperfect; fut. future; fut.ᴘ future passive; aor.ᵃ athematic aorist; aor.ᵗ thematic aorist; aor.ˢ sigmatic aorist; aor.ᴘ aorist passive; per. perfect; plu. pluperfect; cond. conditional.

TABLE I

INDO-EUROPEAN LANGUAGES

I	*Greek*		Ancient Greek	Byzantine Greek	Modern Greek
2	*Italic*		Latin Faliscan	Low Latin	Romance Languages
3			Oscan Umbrian		
4	*Celtic*	*Gaelic*		Old Irish	Irish Scots Gaelic
5		*Cymric*		Old Welsh Old Breton	Welsh Breton
6	*Germanic*	*N. Germanic*		Old Norse	Swedish Danish
7					Norwegian Icelandic
8		*W. Germanic*		Old English Old Frisian	English Frisian
9				Old Low Franconian	Dutch
10				Old High German	German

TABLE I   INDO-EUROPEAN LANGUAGES   59

11	*Baltic*		Old Lithuanian	Lithuanian
12			Old Prussian	
13 *Balto-Slavonic*		*S. Slavonic*	Old Church Slavonic	Bulgarian Serbo-Croat
14	*Slavic*	*W. Slavonic*		Czech,Slovak Polish
15		*E. Slavonic*		Russian Ukrainian
16	*Indic*	Sanskrit	Pali Prakrit	Bengali Hindi
Indo-Iranian 17	*Iranian*	Avestan Old Persian	Pahlavi	Afghan Persian
18 *Armenian*			Old Armenian	Armenian
19 *Albanian*				Albanian
20 *Hittite*				

Note.

   1. Languages still spoken are given in the right-hand column; languages known only from written records in the second and third columns from the right; names written in italic refer to groups of languages.

TABLE II

COMPARATIVE LINGUISTICS

A. *IE Equations*

	English	Latin	Greek	IE	English	Latin	Greek	IE
1	father	pater	πατήρ	*pətēr	ten	decem	δέκα	*dekm̥
2	kin	genus	γένος	*genos	sweet	suauis	ἡδύς	*swād-
3	ewe	ouis	ὄις	*owis	cow	bos	βοῦς	*gʷōus
4	wit	uideo	ἴδον	*wid-	yoke	iugum	ζυγόν	*yug-
5	six	sex	ἕξ	*s(w)eks	snow	niuem	νίφα	*snigʷh-
6	bear	fero	φέρω	*bher-	door	foris	θύρα	*dhur-

B. *Romance Equations*

	French	Italian	Latin	French	Italian	Latin
1	nuit	notte	noctem	bon	buono	bonum
2	fait	fatto	factum	feu	fuoco	focum
3	chose	cosa	causam	épouse	sposa	sponsam
4	loi	legge	legem	épée	spada	spatham
5	clair	chiaro	clarum	ciel	cielo	caelum

TABLE III   THE ALPHABET

	Egyptian	Phoenician	Greek	Latin	Chinese
1	ox-head	aleph	A α ἄλφα	A	牛
2	house	beth	B β βῆτα	B	
3	corner	gimel	Γ γ γάμμα	C, G	
4	door	daleth	Δ δ δέλτα	D	門
5	rejoice	he	E ε εἶ	E	
6	prop Y	vau		F	
7		zayin	Z ζ ζῆτα	Z	
8		cheth	H η ἦτα	H	
9		teth	Θ θ θῆτα		
10	hand	yod	I ι ἰῶτα	I	又
11	plant	kaph	K κ κάππα	K	艸
12	cord	lamed	Λ λ λάμβδα	L	
13	water	mem	M μ μῦ	M	水
14	snake	nun	N ν νῦ	N	
15	fish	samekh	Ξ ξ ξεῖ		魚
16	eye	'ayin	O o οὖ	O	目
17	mouth	pe	Π π πεῖ	F	口
18		qoph		Q	
19	head	resh	P ρ ῥῶ	R	首
20	hill	shin	Σ ς σ σίγμα	S	山
21	cross	tau	T τ ταῦ	T	
22			Y υ ὖ	V, Y	
23			Φ φ φεῖ		
24			X χ χεῖ	X	
25			Ψ ψ ψεῖ		
26			Ω ω ὦ		

Notes. 1. For the Phoenician letters see Buck CGGL p. 69.

    2. Some Chinese characters with the same meanings are given in the right-hand column to illustrate the pictographic origins.

    3. The small letters of both alphabets are in origin simply cursive forms of the capitals, adapted for writing on papyrus and parchment.

    4. Greek sigma has two forms: σ initial and medial, ς final.

TABLE IV

PHONOLOGY (IE AND AG)

A. *IE Vowels*   *AG Vowels* (*Attic*)

	Simple	Diphthongs		Simple		Diphthongs			
				Short	Long				
1	a	ai āi	au āu	α	ᾱ	αι	αυ	ᾳ	
2	e	ei ēi	eu ēu	ε	η	ει	ευ	ῃ	ηυ
3	o	oi ōi	ou ōu	o	ω	οι		ῳ	
4	i			ι	ῑ				
5	u				ου				
6	ə								
7				υ	ῡ	υι			

B.   *IE and AG Consonants*

		Stop				Spirant		Nasal	Liquid		So-nant
		Voiced		Unvoiced		V.	Unv.	Voiced	La-teral	Pa-latal	
		Plain	Asp.	Plain	Asp.						
1	Labial	b β	bh -	p π	ph φ	w -	wh -	m μ			m̥ -
2	Dental	d δ	dh -	t τ	th θ			n ν	l λ	r ρ	n̥ l̥ r̥ -
3	Velar	g γ	gh -	k χ	kh χ	y -		ng γγ γχ			
4	Labio-velar	gʷ -	gʷh -	kʷ -							
5	Sibilant					z ζ s σ					

Tables IV A and IV B are descriptive, not historical; that is, the sounds of IE and AG are classified phonetically. The correspondences between them do not necessarily represent historical relationships.

TABLE IV PHONOLOGY (IE AND AG) 63

C. *Attic Vowel Contractions*

1	⟶	α	ε	ει	ι	η	ῃ	ο	ου	οι	ω	ῳ
2	α	α	α	ᾳ	αι	α	ᾳ	ω	ω	ῳ	ω	ῳ
3	ε	η	ει	ει	ει	η	ῃ	ου	ου	οι	ω	ῳ
4	ο	ω	ου	οι	οι	ω	οι	ου	ου	οι	ω	ῳ

The first vowel is given in the left-hand column, the second in the top row, the resultant contraction where they intersect, e.g. $α + ι = αι$.

D. *Attic Consonant Combinations*

1	⟶	τ	δ	θ	μ	σ	π	β	φ	κ	γ	χ	σθ	ρ
2	π	ππ	βδ	φθ	μμ	ψ							φθ	πρ
3	β	ππ		φθ	μμ	ψ							φθ	βρ
4	φ	ππ	βδ	φθ	μμ	ψ							φθ	φρ
5	κ	κτ	γδ	χθ	γμ	ξ				κκ		κχ	χθ	κρ
6	γ	κτ	γδ	χθ	γμ	ξ							χθ	γρ
7	χ	κτ	γδ	χθ	γμ	ξ							χθ	χρ
8	τ			τθ		σ								τρ
9	δ	στ		σθ		σ								δρ
10	θ	στ		σθ		σ								θρ
11	ν	ντ	νδ	νθ	μμ	ν, σ	μπ	μβ	μφ	γκ	γγ	γχ		νδρ
12	ρ	ρτ	ρδ	ρθ	ρμ	ρρ	ρπ	ρβ	ρφ	ρκ	ργ	ρχ	ρθ	ρρ

To be read as Table IV C.

Notes.

A. 1. The diphthongs ᾳ ῃ ῳ were written αι ηι ωι in AG; in HG they were written and pronounced α η ω; the forms ᾳ ῃ ῳ ('iota subscript') were introduced in BG as an orthographical convention.

2. AG ει had originally two values, (1) long closed e as in φίλει < φίλεε

6

and (2) the true diphthong ει as in γένει < γένε·ϊ; in late Attic both were assimilated to η.

3. AG ου was originally long closed o (Eng. boat), but in Attic it became ū (Eng. boot), while Att. υ (originally u ū as in Latin) acquired the value of French u, German ü.

B. 4. AG φ θ χ were pronounced as in Eng. up*h*old hot*h*ouse ink*h*orn.

5. AG ζ was a double consonant, originally zd (cf. Ἀθήναζε < *Ἀθή-νασ·δε), in Attic dz.

6. AG γγ γκ γχ were pronounced as in Eng. li*n*ger si*n*k i*n*k*h*orn.

C. 7. Att. εα and εο remain uncontracted in certain conditions, e.g. ἡδέα but ἄστη, ῥέω ῥεῖς ῥεῖ ῥέομεν ῥεῖτε ῥέουσι.

8. Vowel contraction may also occur between words, especially when the definite article ὁ τό τά, or the conjunction καί, is followed by a word beginning with α- ε- ο- (crasis): ὁ ἀνήρ ἁνήρ, ὁ ἐμός οὑμός, τὸ αὐτό ταὐτό, τὸ ὄνομα τοὔνομα, τὰ ἄλλα τἆλλα, ἃ ἔχω ἄχω, καὶ ἐγώ κἀγώ, καὶ ἐμοί κἀμοί, καὶ εἶτα κᾆτα, καὶ οὐ κοὐ, καὶ ὅπως χὤπως. Att. ἅτερος θἅτερον stand for ὁ ἅτερος, τὸ ἅτερον (ἅτερος being a by-form of ἕτερος).

D. 9. γμ < κμ χμ is confined mainly to verb stems: διώκω διωγμός, δέχομαι δέδεγμαι. PG νρ > νδρ (ἀνδρός) but AG νρ > ρρ (συρρέω).

TABLE V PHONOLOGY (AG AND MG)

	AG	MG	Examples
1	α ᾱ ᾳ	α	καλά, ὥρα, τώρα (<τῇ ὥρᾳ)
2	αι ε	ε	φαίνεται δένεται δένετε
3	η ει ῃ ι οι υ	ι	λείπει = λύπη, λίγη = λίγοι (< ὀλί-γη ὀλίγοι), πολλή = πολύ = πολλοί
4	ο ω ῳ	ο	μόνο ἀνταμώνω
5	ου	ου	
6	αυ, ευ, ηυ	[av af, eu ef, iv]	παύω αὐτός, σαλεύω εὔκολος, ηὖρα
7	ε	sometimes inter-changed with ο	ὄμορφος (ἔμορφος < εὔμορφος), γιοφύρι (γεφύρι), ὀχτρός (ἐχ-τρός)
8	unstressed initial vowels	often lost	πέθανα (ἀπέθανον), γιαλός (αἰγι-αλός), λεύτερος (ἐλεύθερος), μιλῶ (ὁμιλῶ)

	AG	MG	Examples
9	εο, εα, ια	ιό, ιά [yo, ya]	θιός παλιός, ἐννιά, μιά, ἐκκλησιά.
10	ω unstressed	often ου (Eng. boot)	ἔχουμε κουπί ψαλμουδιά
11	β φ	[v, f]	βαγγέλιο (εὐαγγέλιον), παλαβός, φιλόσοφος
12	γ	[gh] before [a, o] [y] before [e, i]	γάμος ἐγώ ἡγούμενος, γένος γίνω
13	δ, θ	[dh] Eng. *then* [th] Eng. *thin*	δέν, 'Αθήνα
14	ζ	[z] Eng. *zeal*	ζῆλος γυρίζω
15	χ	before [a, o] Eng. *hot* before [e, i] Ger. *ich*	χαρά ἔχω, χαίρω ἔχετε
16	γμ, [vm]	μ	πρᾶμα θαμάζω, ψέμα
17	γκ, μπ, ντ	Eng. li*nger* a*mber* ci*nder*; initial g-, b-, d-	ἀνάγκη λαμπάδα δόντι, γκρεμίζω μπαίνω ντύνω
18	κτ χθ, πτ φθ	χτ, φτ	ὀχτώ ἐδέχτηκα, ἐφτά ἐσκέφτηκα
19	σχ, σθ	σκ, στ	σκίζω γελάστηκα
20	γχ, μφ, νθ	χ, φ, θ	συχωρῶ νύφη πεθερός
21	λλ μμ νν ρρ σσ	λ μ ν ρ σ	
22	-ν final	often lost	ἔχουμε μόνο λόγο, τὴ μέρα
23	'(breathing)	lost	ἕτοιμος == ἕτυμος

Note.

1. In the MG standard language many literary forms have been restored, e.g. θεός, θαυμάζω, αἰσθάνομαι.

2. The AG sounds represented by αι ει οι β γ δ, which disappeared in HG, reappeared later as a result of other phonetic changes: MG ἀηδόνι λέει ρολόι μπαίνω γκρινιάζω ντροπή < AG ἀηδών λέγει ὡρολόγιον ἐμβαίνω ἐγκρίνω ἐντροπή.

TABLE VI
THE SUBSTANTIVE
A. *Basic Endings*

	Sg.					Pl.				
	N	V	A	G	D	NV	A	G	D	
I	-s	×	-m̥	-os, [-syo]	-i	-es, [-i]	-n̥s	-ōm, [-āsōm]	-si, -s	

B. *Athematic*

		Sg.					Pl.				
	N	V	A	G	D	NV	A	G	D	
1	παῖ·ς	παῖ	παῖδ-α	-ός	-ί	-ες	-ας	-ων	παισί	child mf.
2	φύλαξ	~~~~	φύλακ-α	-ος	-ι	-ες	-ας	-ων	φύλαξι	guard m.
3	ῥήτωρ	ῥῆτορ	ῥήτορ-α	-ος	-ι	-ες	-ας	-ων	-σι	speaker m.
4	δαίμων	δαῖμον	δαίμον-α	-ος	-ι	-ες	-ας	-ων	δαίμο·σι	god m.
5	λέων	~~~~	λέοντ-α	-ος	-ι	-ες	-ας	-ων	λέουσι	lion m.
6	σῶμα	~~~~	~~~~	σώματ-ος	-ι	-α	-α	-ων	σώμασι	body n.
7	ἱερ-εύς	-εῦ	-ῆα / -έᾱ	-ῆος / -έως	-ῆι / -εῖ	-ῆες / -εῖς	-ῆας / -έᾱς	-ήων / -έων	-εῦσι	priest m.
8	Σωκράτ-ης	-ες	-ε·α / -η	-ε·ος / -ους	-ε·ι / -ει	-ε·ες / -εις	-ε·ας / -εις	-έ·ων	-ε·σι	Socrates m.
9	γένος	~~~~	~~~~	γένε-ος / γέν-ους	-ι / -ει	-α / -η	-α / -η	-ων / -ῶν	-σι / -ε·σι	kind n.
10	αἰδ-ώς	~~~~	-όα / -ῶ	-όος / -οῦς	-όι / -οῖ					shame f.
11	πατήρ	πάτερ	πατέρ·α	πατρ·ός	-ί	πατέρ-ες	-ας	-ων	πατράσι	father m.
12	ἀνήρ	ἄνερ	ἄνδρ-α	-ός	-ί	-ες	-ας	-ῶν	ἀνδράσι	man m.

TABLE VI   THE SUBSTANTIVE   67

C. *Stems in* -υ -ε -ι

N	V	A	G	D	NV	A	G	D	
πῆχ-υ·ς	-υ	-υ·ν	-ε·ος	-ει	-ε·ες -εις	-εις	-ε·ων	-ε·σι	arm m.
ἰχθ·ύ-ς	×	-ν	-ος	-ι	-ες	-ς -ας	-ων	-σι	fish m.
ἄστ-υ	﹀﹀﹀	﹀﹀﹀	-ε·ος -ε·ως	-ει	-ε·α -η	-ε·α -η	-ε·ων	-ε·σι	town n.
πόλ-ι·ς	πόλ-ι	-ι·ν	-η·ος -ε·ως	-η·ι -ει	-η·ες ΄-εις	-η·ας -εις	-ε·ων	-ε·σι	city f.

(Sg. spans N V A G D; Pl. spans NV A G D)

D. *Thematic* (ο/ε, ᾱ/α)

N	V	A	G	D	NV	A	G	D	
λόγ-ο·ς	-ε	-ο·ν	-οιο -οο -ου	-ῳ	-οι	-ους	-ων	-οισι -οις	word m.
νη-ό·ς νε-ώς	-ε ﹀﹀﹀	-ό·ν -ώ·ν	-οῖο -όο -ῶ	-ῷ -ῷ	-οί -ῴ	-ούς -ώς	-ῶν -ῶν	-οῖσι -ῷς	shrine m.
πλοῖ-ο·ν	﹀﹀﹀	-ο·ν	-οιο -οο -ου	-ῳ	-α	-α	-ων	-οισι -οις	boat n.
ὥρ-η ὥρ-α	﹀﹀﹀ ﹀﹀﹀	-ην -ᾱν	-ης -ᾱς	-η -ᾳ	-αι	-ᾱς	-άων -ῶν	-ῇσι -αις	season f.
λύπ-η	﹀﹀﹀	-ην	-ης	-η	-αι	-ᾱς	-άων -ῶν	-ῇσι -αις	grief f.
σφαῖρ-α	﹀﹀﹀	-αν	-ης ·-ᾱς	-η -ᾳ	-αι	-ᾱς	-άων -ῶν	-ησι -αις	ball f.
χλαῖν-α	﹀﹀﹀	-αν	-ης	-η	-αι	-ᾱς	-άων -ῶν	-ησι -αις	cloak f.
ταμί-ης ταμί-ᾱς	-η -ᾱ	-ην -ᾱν	-ᾱο -εω -ου	-η -ᾳ	-αι	-ᾱς	-άων -ῶν	-ησι -αις	steward m.
ναύτ-ης	-α	-ην	-ᾱο -εω -ου	-η	-αι	-ᾱς	-άων -ῶν	-ησι -αις	sailor m.

Notes.

A. I. The bracketed forms belonged originally to the pronoun.

2. The ending -si was in origin a locative ('Ἀθήνη·σι 'at Athens'), the ending -s an instrumental. They were transferred to the true dat. in PG.

B. 3. In the nom. sg. and dat. pl. of athematic stems the final consonant of the stem combines with the following σ according to the laws of consonant assimilation: Table IV D.

4. Acc. sg. -α < -μ: XI.3.5; dat. pl. παισί < *παιδ·σί: XI.3.13.

5. In nominatives of the type ῥήτωρ δαίμων λέων the ending -ς had probably been lost in IE.

6. Dat. pl. δαίμοσι for *δαιμασι < *δαιμν·σι, λέουσι < *λεον·σι < *λεοντ·σι: XI.3.16.

7. NVA. sg. σῶμα < *σωμντ: XI.3.8.

8. ἱερεύς-εῦ-ῆα < *ἱερ·ηϜς -ηϜ -ηϜα, with vocalisation or loss of Ϝ: hence acc. sg. -α, not -ν. Att. ἱερ·έᾱ -έως -έᾱς for ἱερ-ῆα -ῆος -ῆας by quantitative metathesis: XI.3.14.

9. Σωκράτης γένος αἰδώς: the stems are Σωκρατεσ- γενεσ- αἰδοσ- with loss of intervocalic -σ-: XI.3.7.

10. Att. Ion. dat. pl. γένεσι < γένεσσι.

11. πατήρ ἀνήρ with radical vowel gradation πατήρ / πάτερ / πατρ-, ἀνήρ / ἄνερ / ἀνδρ- (< *ἀνρ: Table IV D): dat. pl. πατράσι ἀνδράσι < *πατρ·σι *ἀνρ·σι.

12. Besides the Att. Ion. dat. pl. in -σι Epic has the Aeo. dat. pl. in -εσσι (παίδεσσι) formed from the type γένεσ·σι by analogy, the disyllable -εσσι being taken as the ending.

C. 13. C 1-4 are properly athematic stems in -w or -y, with radical vowel gradation except in no. 2 (*pāchw- *pāchwe-, *poly- *polye-).

14. Att. acc. pl. πήχεις < *πηχ·ε·νς, ἰχθῦς < *ἰχθ·υ·νς (XI.3.16); later ἰχθύας with -ας on the analogy of παῖδας etc.

15. ἄστυ: Att. gen. sg. ἄστεως on the analogy of πόλεως.

16. πόλις: Att. gen. sg. πόλεως < πόληος: XI.3.14.

D. 17. Substantives of the type λόγος are mostly masculine, but not all: παρθένος f. 'maiden', νῆσος f. 'island' etc. The association of this type with the masculine gender began with adjectives of the type σοφ-ός -ή -όν (Table VII). Substantives of the types ὥρα and σφαῖρα are exclusively feminine; but the type ὥρα was originally of common gender, as in Latin mensa nauta, and some dialects preserved the old nom. sg. ταμίᾱ ναύτᾱ for ταμί-ᾱς (-ης) ναύτ-ᾱς (-ης): see 22.

18. λόγος: gen. sg. λόγου < λόγ·ο·ο < λόγ·οιο < *λογο·σγο; acc. pl. λόγους < λόγονς: XI.3.16. So Att. πλοῦς < πλόος with vowel contraction (Table IV C).

TABLE VI   THE SUBSTANTIVE   69

19. Att. νεώς < νηός < ναός: XI.3.14.
20. Epic -η (< IE ā) = Att. -η or -ᾱ according to position: XI.3.2; Epic gen. pl. -άων (> Att. -ῶν) < -ᾱσων, also -έων < -ήων < -άων.
21. σφαῖρα χλαῖνα< *σφαρυα *χλανυα, cf. μέλαινα< *μελανυα (Table VII), and so with all nouns of this type, which was originally an independent one but in Greek was merged partly with the type ὥρα.
22. ταμί·ᾱ·ς ναύτ·ᾱ·ς (> ναύτης) have borrowed the -ς from λόγ·ο·ς. Similarly, in the gen. sg., Epic -εω < -ηο < -αο has borrowed the -ο from λόγ·οιο, and Att. -ου is from λόγ·ου: see 17.
23. Dual. The dual forms of the noun are: (1) NVA παῖδ·ε πήχ·ει (< πήχε·ε), GD παίδ·οιν πηχ·έ·οιν, (2) NVA λόγ·ω λύπ·ᾱ etc. (3) GD λόγ·οιν λύπ·αιν etc.

TABLE VII

THE ADJECTIVE

Sg.					Pl.				
N	V	A	G	D	NV	A	G	D	
πᾶς	∿∿∿	πάντ-α	-ός	-ί	-ες	-ας	-ων	πᾶσι	every, all
πᾶσ-α	∿∿∿	-αν	-ης	-η	-αι	-ᾱς	-ῶν	-αις	
πᾶν	∿∿∿	∿∿∿	παντ-ός	-ί	-α	-α	-ων	πᾶσι	
μέλᾱς	∿∿∿	μέλαν-α	-ος	-ι	-ες	-ας	-ων	μέλασι	
μέλαιν-α	∿∿∿	-αν	-ης	-η	-αι	-ᾱς	-ῶν	-αις	black
μέλαν	∿∿∿	∿∿∿	μέλαν-ος	-ι	-α	-α	-ων	μέλασι	
ἄφρων	ἄφρον	ἄφρον-α	-ος	-ι	-ες	-ας	-ων	ἄφροσι	foolish
ἄφρον	∿∿∿	∿∿∿	ἄφρον-ος	-ι	-α	-α	-ων		
σαφ-ής	-ές	-ῆ	-οῦς	-εῖ	-εῖς	-εῖς	-έων	-έσι	clear
σαφ-ές	∿∿∿	∿∿∿			-ῆ	-ῆ			
βαρ-ύ·ς	∿∿∿	-ύ·ν	-έ·ος	-εῖ	-εῖς	-εῖς	-έ·ων	-έ·σι	
βαρ·εῖ-α	∿∿∿	-αν	-ᾱς	-ᾳ	-αι	-ᾱς	-ῶν	-αις	heavy
βαρ-ύ	∿∿∿	∿∿∿	-έ·ος	-εῖ	-έ·α	-έ·α	-έ·ων	έ·σι	
σοφ-ό·ς	∿∿∿	-ό·ν	-οῦ	-ῷ	-οί	-ούς	-ῶν	-οῖς	
σοφ-ή	∿∿∿	-ή·ν	-ῆς	-ῆ	-αί	-ᾱς	-ῶν	-αῖς	wise
σοφ-ό·ν	∿∿∿	∿∿∿	-οῦ	-ῷ	-ά	-ά	-ῶν	-οῖς	

Notes.

1. Only the Attic forms are given here; the Epic forms can be deduced from Table VI.
2. πᾶς (m.) πᾶσα (f.) πᾶν (n.) is an adjective of three terminations; so

μέλας, βαρύς, σοφός: ἄφρων (mf.) ἄφρον (n.) and σαφής (mf.) σαφές (n.) are adjectives of two terminations.

3. πᾶς < *παντ·ς like παῖς < *παιδ·ς, πᾶσα < *πανσα < *παντγα like χλαῖνα < *χλανγα, πᾶν < *παντ like σῶμα < *σωμντ.

4. μέλας μέλαινα μέλαν < *μελαν·ς *μελαν·γα μέλαν. Dat. pl. μέλασι on the analogy of μέλανι μέλανες etc.

5. ἄφρων like δαίμων.

6. σαφής (stem σαφέ- < σαφέσ-) like Σωκράτης.

7. βαρύς like πῆχυς, βαρεῖα like σφαῖρα, βαρύ like ἄστυ. In contrast to ἄστη the neut. pl. βαρέα remains uncontracted.

8. σοφός like λόγος, σοφή like λύπη, σοφόν like πλοῖον. Many adjectives of this class, especially compounds, have two terminations only, e.g. ἄφιλος (mf.) ἄφιλον (n.) 'friendless'. Contracted: ἁπλοῦς (< ἁπλόος: Table VI.18) ἁπλῆ ἁπλοῦν 'simple', with -ῆ in sg.f. and -ᾶ in pl.n. NVA by analogy with σοφή σοφά.

9. The IE suffixes of comparison were (1) -yes- / -yos- / -is- comparative, and (2) -isto- / -iste- superlative, both added to the root, not to the stem of the adjective. Hence AG αἰσχ·ρ-ός 'shameful': (1) comparative nom. sg. mf. *αἰσχιως, n. *αἰσχιος (cf. Lat. -ior -ius), acc. sg. mf. αἰσχίω (< *αἰσχιοσα), gen. sg. αἰσχίους (< *αἰσχιοσος), nom. pl. mf. αἰσχίους (< *αἰσχιοσες), n. αἰσχίω (< *αἰσχιοσα); (2) superlative αἴσχιστ-ος -η -ον. The comparative nom. sg. was reconstructed with an element -ν- as mf. αἰσχίων, n. αἴσχιον, and on this basis a new stem αἰσχίον- was created, hence mf. αἰσχίων n. αἴσχιον, like ἄφρων. Another mode of comparison, which became in AG the only productive one, was based on the elements -τερ- (comparative) and -τατ- (superlative) added to the stem of the adjective: μελάντερ-ος -α -ον 'blacker', μελάντατ-ος -η -ον 'blackest'; σαφέστερ-ος -α -ον 'clearer', σαφέστατ-ος -η -ον 'clearest'; βαρύτερ-ος -α -ον 'heavier', βαρύτατ-ος -η -ον 'heaviest'; σοφώτερ-ος -α -ον 'wiser', σοφώτατ-ος -η -ον 'wisest'. In adjectives of the type σοφός the quantity of the theme-vowel varied inversely according to the metrical length of the preceding syllable: σοφός σοφώτερος σοφώτατος but δεινός 'strange' δεινότερος δεινότατος, μακρός 'long' μακρότερος μακρότατος.

10. Adverbs were formed in various ways, the commonest being the suffix -ως (-ω ablative with suffix -ς): πάντως ἀφρόνως σαφῶς βαρέως σοφῶς. For the comparative the acc. sg. n. of the adjective was used (σαφέστερον etc.); for the superlative, the acc. pl. n. (σαφέστατα etc.).

TABLE VIII

THE PRONOUN

	Sg.				Pl.				
	N	A	G	D	N	A	G	D	
1			μεο ἐμεῦ				ἡμέας	ἡμέων		
2	ἐγώ	με ἐμέ		μοι ἐμοί	ἡμεῖς				ἡμῖν	I
3			μου ἐμοῦ			ἡμᾶς	ἡμῶν		
4			σεο σεῦ	τοι τοί		ὑμέας	ὑμέων			
5	σύ	σε σέ			ὑμεῖς				ὑμῖν	thou
6			σου σοῦ	σοι σοί		ὑμᾶς	ὑμῶν		
7		ἑ ἕ	ἑο ἕο	οἱ οἷ		σφέας	σφέων	σφίσι	him
8		αὐτ-όν	-οῦ	-ῷ		-ούς		-οῖς	him,
9		αὐτ-ήν	-ῆς	-ῇ		-ᾱς	-ῶν	-αῖς	her,
0		αὐτ-ό	-οῦ	-ῷ		-ά		-οῖς	it
1	ὁ	τόν	τοῦ	τῷ	οἱ	τούς		τοῖς	that,
2	ἡ	τήν	τῆς	τῇ	αἱ	τάς	τῶν	ταῖς	the
3	τό	τό	τοῦ	τῷ	τά	τά		τοῖς
4	ὅδε	τόνδε	τοῦδε	τῷδε	οἵδε	τούσδε		τοῖσδε	
5	ἥδε	τήνδε	τῆσδε	τῇδε	αἵδε	τάσδε	τῶνδε	ταῖσδε	that
6	τόδε	τόδε	τοῦδε	τῷδε	τάδε	τάδε		τοῖσδε
7	οὗτ·ος	τοῦτ-ον	-ου	-ῳ	οὗτοι	τούτους		τούτοις	
8	αὕτ·η	ταύτ-ην	-ης	-ῃ	αὗται	ταύτᾱς	τούτων	ταύταις	this
9	τοῦτ-ο	wwww	-ου	-ῳ	ταῦτα	ταῦτα		τούτοις
0	ὅς	ὅν	οὗ	ᾧ	οἵ	οὕς		οἷς	who
1	ἥ	ἥν	ἧς	ᾗ	αἵ	ἅς	ὧν	αἷς	which
2	ὅ	ὅ	οὗ	ᾧ	ἅ	ἅ		οἷς
3	τίς (mf.)	τίνα			τίν-ες	-ας			who?
4			τίνος τοῦ	τίνι τῷ			-ων	τίσι	what?
5	τί (n.)	τί			τίν-α	-α		
6	τις (mf.)	τινά			τιν-ές	-άς			some-one
7			τινός του	τινί τῳ			τινῶν	τισί	
8	τι (n.)	τι			ἄττα	ἄττα			some-thing

Notes.

1. The forms ἐγώ με, σύ σε, ἑ have no endings; the nom. acc. sg. n. in -ο (< *-οδ, Lat. -ud) is distinctive of the pronoun; so, originally were

the nom. pl. mf. endings in -οι -αι, the gen. sg. in -ε·ο -ου (< *e·syo), and the gen. pl. in -ῶν < -άων, but these have spread to the noun; see Table VI.1.

2. The nom. of the personal pronouns is only used when the pronoun is emphatic: τί θέλεις σύ; 'what do *you* want?' For the third person one of the demonstrative pronouns is used: τί θέλει οὗτος; 'what does *he* want?' The unaccented forms of the personal pronouns με σε ἑ etc. are enclitic and unemphatic (VI.4). In Aftic ἑ etc. and σφέας etc. were replaced by αὐτ-όν -ήν -ό. In addition, αὐτ-ός -ή -ό has the following uses: (1) predicatively, τί θέλεις αὐτός; 'what do you want yourself?', εἶδον αὐτὸν τὸν ἄνδρα 'I saw the man himself'; (2) attributively, preceded by the definite article, εἶδον τὸν αὐτὸν ἄνδρα 'I saw the same man'; (3) in combination with the personal pronouns as a reflexive: ἐμαυτ-όν -ήν, -οῦ -ῆς, -ῷ -ῇ, ἡμᾶς αὐτούς (αὐτάς), ἡμῶν αὐτῶν, ἡμῖν αὐτοῖς (αὐταῖς); so σεαυτ-όν -ήν etc. (also σαυτ-όν -ήν); ἑαυτ-όν -ήν -ό etc. (also αὐτ-όν -ήν -ό etc.): μὴ βλάπτε σεαυτόν 'don't hurt yourself'. HG gives ἑαυτόν etc. for all persons.

4. The pronoun ὁ ἡ τό was originally a demonstrative (as commonly in Epic) but in CG it became the definite article, cf. French le la (Lat. illum illam); ὅδε ἥδε τόδε is the same word with the demonstrative suffix -δε; so τοιόσ·δε τοιά·δε τοιόν·δε 'such', τοσόσ·δε τοσή·δε τοσόν·δε 'so much'.

5. The demonstrative οὗτος αὕτη τοῦτο is compounded of ὁ ἡ τό and forms related to αὐτ-ός -ή -ό, but its precise origin is obscure; so τοιοῦτος τοιαύτη τοιοῦτο 'such', τοσοῦτος τοσαύτη τοσοῦτο 'so much', τηλικοῦτος τηλικαύτη τηλικοῦτο 'of this age'.

6. The pronominal nom. sg. n. in -ο (Lat. -ud) appears also in (ἐ)κεῖν-ος -η -ο 'that' and ἄλλ-ος -η -ο (< *ἄλγος = Lat. alius).

7. The interrogative τίς and the indefinite τις are in origin the same word, the latter being enclitic. It was originally a thematic ι/ε stem: sg. nom. τις τι, acc. *τιν τι, gen. τεο pl. nom. n. *τγα, gen. τεων, dat. τισι. The acc. sg. mf. τινα was formed from *τιν on the analogy of ἕνα (10), and hence the forms τιν-ος τιν-ι etc. with τιν- as the stem. The dat. sg. τῳ was formed after the gen. sg. του. The pl. n. ἄττα was perhaps formed by false division from *τγα under the influence of such combinations as ἄλλ' ἄττα for ἄλλα ττα (*ττα < *τγα).

8. The indefinite relative 'whoever' has two forms: (1) ὅσ·τις ἥ·τις ὅ·τι, compounded from ὅς ἥ ὅ and τις τι, both elements being declined throughout (ὅν·τινα οὗ·τινος etc.); (2) ὅ·τις ὅ·τι, ὅ·τινα ὅ·τι, ὅ·του ὅ·τῳ, based on ὅ·τι: in this form only the second element is declined.

TABLE VIII   THE PRONOUN   73

9. The reciprocal ἀλλήλ-ους -ας -α, -ων, -οις -αις -οις arose out of such combinations as ἄλλοι ἄλλους, ἄλλαι ἄλλας.

10. The first four numerals are declinable: (1) εἷς μία ἕν (< *sems *smya *sem), acc. ἕνα μίαν ἕν (ἕνα for *ἕμα by analogy with ἕν); (2) NVA δύω δύο, GD δυοῖν, (or δύο indeclinable); (3) τρεῖς τρία (*treyes *trya) τριῶν, τρισί; (4) Att. τέτταρ-ες -α, τεττάρ·ων, τέτταρ·σι.

TABLE IX
THE VERB: PERSONAL ENDINGS (ACTIVE)
A. *Basic Endings.*   B. φημί *say.*   C. λείπω *leave,* λύω *loose*

		Sg.			Pl.		
		1	2	3	1	2	3
A. 1	Pri.	-o·mi	-e·si	-e·ti	-o·men	-e·te	-o·nti
2	Sec.	-o·m	-e·s	-e·t	-o·men	-e·te	-o·nt
B. 1	Ind. pre.	φη-μί	-ις	-σί	φα-μέν	-τέ	φᾱσί
2	aor.ᵃ	ἔ·φη-ν	-ς	✕	ἔ·φα-μεν	-τε	-ν -σαν
3	Opt.	φα·ί-η·ν	-η·ς	-η	-μεν	-τε	-ε·ν
4	Imp.	φά-	-θι	-τ·ω		-τε	-ν·των
C. 1	Ind. pre.	λείπ-ω λύ-ω	-εις	-ει	-o·μεν	-ε·τε	-ουσι
2	fut.	λείψ-ω λύ·σ-ω	-εις	-ει	-o·μεν	-ε·τε	-ουσι
3	impf.	ἔ·λειπ-ο·ν ἔ·λυ-ο·ν	-ε·ς	-ε	-o·μεν	-ε·τε	-o·ν
4	aor.ᵗ	ἔ·λιπ-ο·ν	-ε·ς	-ε	-o·μεν	-ε·τε	-o·ν
5	aor.ˢ	ἔ·λυ·σ-α	-α·ς	-ε	-α·μεν	-α·τε	-α·ν
6	aor.ᵖ	ἐ·λείφ·θ-η·ν ἐ·λύ·θ-η·ν	-η·ς	-η	-η·μεν	η·τε	-ε·ν / -η·σαν
7	per.	λέ·λοιπ-α λέ·λυ·κ-α	-α·ς	-ε	-α·μεν	-α·τε	-ᾱσι
8	plu.	ἐ·λε·λοίπ-η ἐ·λε·λύ·κ-η	-η·ς	-ει	-ε·μεν	-ε·τε	-ε·σαν
9	Sub. pre.	λείπ-ω λύ-ω	-ης	-η	-ω·μεν	-η·τε	-ω·σι
10	aorᵗʰ.	λίπ-ω λύ·σ-ω	-ης	-η	-ω·μεν	-η·τε	-ω·σι
11	aor.ᵖ	λειφ·θ-ῶ λυ·θ-ῶ	-ῆς	-ῇ	-ῶ·μεν	-ῆ·τε	-ῶ·σι
12	Opt. pre.	λείπ·οι-μι λύ·οι-μι	-ς	✕	-μεν	-τε	-ε·ν

—continued on p. 76

TABLE IX
THE VERB: PERSONAL ENDINGS (MEDIO-PASSIVE)

A. *Basic Endings.*   B. φάμαι   C. λείπομαι, λύομαι

		Sg.			Pl.		
		1	2	3	1	2	3
1	Pri.	-o·mai	-e·sai	-e·tai	-o·metha	-e·sthe	-o·ntai
2	Sec.	-o·mān	-e·so	-e·to	-o·metha	-e·sthe	-o·nto
1	Ind. pre.	*φά-μαι	-σαι	-ται	-μεθα	-σθε	-νται
2	aor.ᵃ	ἐ·φά-μην	-σο	-το	-μεθα	-σθε	-ντο
3	Opt.	*φαί-μην	-ο	-το	-μεθα	-σθε	-ατο -ντο
4	Imp.	*φά-	-σο	-σθω		-σθε	-σθων
1	Ind. pre.	λείπ-ο·μαι λύ-ο·μαι	-ε·αι -η	-ε·ται	-ό·μεθα	-ε·σθε	-ο·νται
2	fut.	λείψ-ο·μαι λύ·σ-ο·μαι	-ε·αι -η	-ε·ται	-ό·μεθα	-ε·σθε	-ο·νται
3	fut.ᴾ	λειφ·θή·σ-ο·μαι λυ·θή·σ-ο·μαι	-ε·αι -η	-ε·ται	-ό·μεθα	-ε·σθε	-ο· νται
4	impf.	ἐ·λειπ-ό·μην ἐ·λυ-ό·μην	-ε·ο -ου	-ε·το	-ό·μεθα	-ε·σθε	-ο·ντο
5	aor.ᵗ	ἐ·λιπ-ό·μην	-ε·ο -ου	-ε·το	-ό·μεθα	-ε·σθε	-ο·ντο
6	aor.ˢ	ἐ·λυ·σ-ά·μην	-α·ο -ω	-α·το	-ά·μεθα	-α·σθε	-α·ντο
7	per.	λέ·λειμ·μαι λέ·λυ-μαι	-σαι	-ται	-μεθα	-σθε	-νται
8	plu.	ἐ·λε·λείμ·μην ἐ·λε·λύ-μην	-σο	-το	-μεθα	-σθε	-ντο
9	Sub. pre.	λείπ-ω·μαι λύ-ω·μαι	-η·αι -η	-η·ται	-ώ·μεθα	-η·σθε	-ω·νται
10	aor.ᵗˢ	λίπ-ω·μαι λύ·σ-ω·μαι	-η·αι -η	-η·ται	-ώ·μεθα	-η·σθε	-ω·νται
11	Opt. pre.	λειπ·οί-μην λυ·οί-μην	-ο	-το	-μεθα	-σθε	-ατο -ντο

—*continued on p* 77

		Sg.			Pl.		
		1	2	3	1	2	3
13	aor.ᵗˢ	λίπ·οι-μι λύ·σ·αι-μι	-ς	×	-μεν	-τε	-ε·ν
14	aor.ᴾ	λειφ·θεί-η·ν λυ·θεί-η·ν	-η·ς	-η	-μεν	-τε	-ε·ν
15	Imp. pre.	λειπ- λυ-	-ε	-έ·τ·ω		-ε·τε	{-ό·ντ·ων {-έ·τω·σαν
16	aor.ᵗ	λιπ-	-ε	-έ·τ·ω		-ε·τε	{-ό·ντ·ων {-έ·τω·σαν
17	aor.ˢ	λυ·σ-	-ο·ν	-ά·τ·ω		-α·τε	{-ά·ντ·ων {-ά·τω·σαν
18	aor.ᴾ	λειφ·θ-	-η·τι	-ή·τ·ω		-η·τε	-έ·ντ·ων

Notes.

A. 1. The primary endings are used for the present, future and perfect indicative and for the subjunctive; the secondary endings are used for the imperfect, aorist and pluperfect indicative and for the optative. The initial vowels are the theme-vowels. The origin of the ending -o·mān (for -o·mo?) is unknown; it may have arisen on the analogy of the athematic aorist ἔφᾶν.

B. 2. Indicative active: these forms are subject to radical vowel gradation, the singular being in the long grade and the plural in the short grade. The corresponding medio-passive forms are in the short grade throughout. The long grade is represented in Attic-Ionic by η < ᾱ: XI.3.2.

3. Indicative active present. Sg. 2 φηίς (written φής) (with -ς borrowed from the aor. sg. 2 ἔ·φη·ς) < *φᾶ·σι (with loss of intervocalic -σ- (XI.3.7)). Sg. 3 φησί < φᾶσι < φᾶτι (with assibilation: XI.3.11). Pl. 3 φᾶσί < φανσί (XI.3.16) < φαντί (XI.3.11).

4. Indicative medio-passive present. Sg. 2 *φάσαι: for the preservation of intervocalic -σ- see 27.

5. Indicative active aorist. Sg. 2 for ἔφης Attic usually gives ἔφησ·θα: -θα is an old per. sg. 2 ending (see 37). Sg. 3 ἔφη < ἐφᾶ < *ἔφᾶτ: XI.3.8. Pl. 3 Ep. ἔ·φα·ν < *ἔ·φα·ντ (XI.3.8), Att. ἔ·φασαν with -σαν borrowed from the sigmatic aorist: see 21.

6. Indicative medio-passive aorist: for ἔφασο see 4, 27.

		Sg.			Pl.		
		I	2	3	I	2	3
12	aor.ⁱˢ	λιπ·οί-μην λυ·σ·αί-μην	-ο	-το	-μεθα	-σθε	$\begin{cases}-α\cdot το\\-ν\cdot το\end{cases}$
13	Imp. pre.	λειπ- λύ-	$\begin{cases}-ε\cdot ο\\-ου\end{cases}$	-έ·σθω		-ε·σθε	-έ·σθων
14	aor.ⁱ	λιπ-	$\begin{cases}-έ\cdot ο\\-οῦ\end{cases}$	-έ·σθω		-έ·σθε	-έ·σθων
15	aor.ˢ	λυ·σ-		-αι	-ά·σθω		-α·σθε	-ά·σθων

7. The optative infix is ι / ιε / ιη. Act. sg. pl. 3 φαίη φαῖεν < *φαιητ *φαιεντ. Mp. pl. 3 Ep. φαίατο, Att. φαῖντο. In the former case the y was treated as a consonant, in the latter as a vowel: see 28.

8. Imperative active. Sg. 2 φάθι: -θι is a suffix added to the verb stem: see 34. Sg. pl. 3 φά·τ·ω φά·ντ·ων: these forms preserve the final -t of the basic endings.

9. Imperative medio-passive. Sg. 2 *φάσο: for the preservation of intervocalic -σ- see 27.

10. There is also a subjunctive φῶ (*φαω) like λυθῶ.

11. There is an aorist passive indicative ἐφάθην, like ἐλύθην; subjunctive φαθῶ, like λυθῶ; optative φαθείην, like λυθείην; imperative *φάθητι, like λύθητι; future active indicative φήσω.

12. There is a perfect medio-passive πέφαμαι, like λέλυμαι.

13. Other verbs of the type φημί have a reduplicated present: ἵ·στη·μι (< *σι·στη·μι) τί·θη·μι (*θι·θη·μι) δί·δω·μι etc.: see Table XI. In these verbs the imperfect (reduplicated) is distinguished from the aorist (not reduplicated): ἵ·στη·ν ἔ·στη·ν, ἐ·τί·θη·ν *ἐ·θη·ν (Att. ἔθηκα).

C. 14. Indicative active present. Sg. 1 λείπ·ω λύ·ω: the -ω is the theme-vowel lengthened, and the ending -μι has been lost; forms of the type λύ·ω·μι are found in Epic but only in the subjunctive. Sg. 2 λείπ·εις λύ·εις: -εις for -ει < -εσι (see above 3). Sg. 3 λείπ·ει λύ·ει: -ει for -ε·τι. These two endings have been remodelled on the analogy of the impf. ἔ·λειπ·ε·ς ἔ·λειπ·ε. Pl. 3 λείπουσι < λείπ·ο·ντι (see above 3).

15. Indicative medio-passive present. Sg. 2 Ep. λείπ·ε·αι < *λείπ·ε·σαι

(IX.3.7), Att. λείπῃ (Table IV C), later λείπει. The -σ- in *λειπ·ε-σαι was lost, because in these verbs, being thematic, it was always intervocalic: see 27.

16. Indicative future. Sg. 1 λείψω λείψομαι < *λειπ·σ·ω *λειπ·σ·ο·μαι: Table IV D. Indicative future passive: for the passive infix -θη- see 23.

17. Indicative active imperfect. Sg. 3 ἔ·λειπ·ε < *ἔ·λειπ·ε·τ. Pl. 3 ἔ·λειπ·ο·ν < *ἔ·λειπ·ο·ντ: XI.3.8.

18. Indicative medio-passive imperfect. Sg. 2 Ep. ἐ·λείπ·ε·ο, Att. ἐ·λείπ·ου < *ἐ·λειπ·ε·σο: see above 15.

19. The thematic aorist has the same endings as the imperfect in the indicative mood; in the other moods it has the same endings as the present; it is distinguished by the form of the stem (λειπ- / λιπ-: IX.1). The middle ἐλιπόμην is middle only, not medio-passive.

20. The sigmatic aorist (type ἔλυσα) was formed from the athematic aorist (type ἔφην) with the infix -σ-: *ἔ·λυ·σ·ν (XI.3.5). Once established, this derivative -α was extended to all the other persons, except the third singular, as a spurious theme-vowel serving to keep the consonants apart; and from the indicative it spread to the optative and imperative (except imp. sg. 2 λῦσον, which is unexplained) and to the infinitive and participle. The third singular ἔλυσε follows the imperfect ἔλυε. The original function of the infix was to make the aorist transitive. A number of verbs have two aorists, athematic and sigmatic, the former intransitive and the latter transitive: ἔστην ἔστησα, ἔβην ἔβησα, ἔδυν ἔδυσα, ἔσβην ἔσβεσα. Apart from these verbs, however, the distinction between the three types of aorist became purely formal, with the sigmatic predominating as the only productive type. The middle ἐλυσάμην is middle only, not medio-passive.

21. Indicative active aorist sigmatic. The pl. 3 ending -σαν spread in Attic to the athematic aorist (ἔφασαν) and aorist passive (ἐλύθησαν) and in HG to the thematic aorist (ἐλάβοσαν) and the imperative (λυέτωσαν for λυόντων): III.5.

22. Indicative middle aorist sigmatic sg. 2 Ep. -αο, Att. -ω: see above 15 and Table IV C.

23. Indicative aorist passive. The type ἐ·λείφ·θη·ν ἐ·λύ·θη·ν was formed with the infix θη / θε from an intransitive aorist active of the type *ἐλιπην *ἐλυην, cf. ἔστην ἔβην ἔδυν etc. (see above 20). Forms of this type are actually found as alternative ('strong')

TABLE IX   THE VERB: PERSONAL ENDINGS   79

forms of the aorist passive: Table XI ἐπάγην ἐπήχθην, ἐτράφην ἐθρέφθην, ἐφάνην ἐφάνθην.

24. Indicative perfect and pluperfect. The infix -κ- appears regularly in vowel stems (λέ·λυ·κα) but not in consonant stems (λέ·λοιπ·α). Some perfects are subject to radical vowel gradation, like the athematic presents (see above 2): γέγον-α -ας -ε γέγα-μεν -τε -ᾱσι (< *γε·γν·μεν -τε: XI.3.5), Att. γεγόν-αμεν -ατε -ᾱσι, so τέθνηκ-α -ας -ε τέθν-αμεν -ατε -ᾱσι. For the ending -ᾱσι see 25.

25. Indicative active perfect sg. 1 -α is an old IE perfect ending, which in PG became associated with the aor.[s] sg. 1 -α (see above 20), and accordingly the other endings were assimilated to those of the sigmatic aorist, except the pl. 3 -ᾱσι (primary, like the pre. -ουσι, as opposed to the secondary -αν). The form -ᾱσι stands for -αντι, formed from -ατι < ντι on the analogy of -ουσι < -οντι.

26. Indicative active pluperfect sg. 1 -η < -εα: Table IV C.

27. Indicative medio-passive perfect and pluperfect sg. 2 λέλυσαι ἐλέλυσο. These forms preserve the -σ-, although it is intervocalic, on the analogy of the consonant stems (λέλειψαι ἐλέλειψο), where it is not intervocalic.

28. Indicative medio-passive perfect and pluperfect pl. 3. Ionic gives λελείπαται ἐλελείπατο (XI.3.5) and these forms were extended by analogy to vowel stems (λελύαται ἐλελύατο); Attic gives λελειμμένοι εἰσί, λελειμμένοι ἦσαν.

29. The ind. mp. per. plu. of consonant stems are subject to the laws of consonant assimilation (Table IV D): λέλειμμαι λέλειψαι λέλειπται λελείμμεθα λέλειφθε, ἐλελείμμην ἐλέλειψο ἐλέλειπτο ἐλελείμμεθα ἐλέλειφθε. For the pl. 3 see 28.

30. The subjunctive was formed from the indicative by lengthening the theme-vowel. In Epic we find also the older 'short-vowel' subjunctive, e.g. ἴ·ο·μεν (Att. ἴωμεν), which stands to the indicative ἴ·μεν as thematic to athematic: IX.5.

31. Subjunctive passive aorist λειφ·θῶ. For the modification of the stem see above 29. The endings -θῶ -θῇς -θῇ etc. are contracted from -θέ·ω -θέ·ης -θέ·η etc.

32. Optative active present and aorist sg. 1: λείποιμι λύοιμι λίποιμι λύσαιμι all have the primary ending -μι in place of the secondary ending -ν. The forms τρέφοιν (for τρέφοιμι) and ἁμάρτοιν (for ἁμάρτοιμι) are attested for early Attic.

33. Opt. act. aor.[s] Attic has the following variants: sg. 2 λύσειας, 3 λύσειε, pl. 3 λύσειαν. They may have arisen through the combined

influence of the opt. aor.ᴾ pl. 3 λύθειεν and the ind. act. aor.ˢ pl. 3 ἔλυσαν.

34. Imperative. The aor.ˢ endings -ον and -αι are unexplained. The imp. aor.ᴾ sg. 2 λείφθητι has the suffix -θι, like φάθι (see above 8) with deaspiration: XI.3.15. In φάθι the -θι is not deaspirated, being protected by the corresponding forms of other verbs στῆθι βῆθι δῦθι etc.

35. There is only one athematic present with a consonant stem, the verb εἰμί (< *ἐσ·μι) 'I am'. The present and imperfect indicative forms are given in Table XIII. The other parts are: indicative future Ep. ἔσσομαι, Att. ἔσομαι (sg. 3 Ep. ἔσσεται, Att. ἔσται); subjunctive Ep. ἔω (< *ἔσω = Lat. ero), Att. ὦ; optative εἴην (<*ἐσγην); imperative sg. ἴσθι (for *σ·θι with prothetic vowel: XI.1) ἔστω, pl. ἔστε ὄντων, infinitive Ep. ἔμμεν, Att. εἶναι (< *ἐσ·ναι); participle Ep. ἐών ἐοῦσα ἐόν, Att. ὤν ουσα ὄν.

36. The verb εἶμι 'go' belongs to the type φημί, but with some peculiar features. Ind. pre. εἶμι εἶ εἶσι ἴμεν ἴτε ἴᾱσι, impf. ᾖα ᾔεις ᾔει ᾖμεν ᾖτε ᾖσαν, sub. ἴω, opt. ἴοιμι, imp. ἴθι ἴτω ἴτε ἰόντων, inf. ἰέναι, ptc. ἰών ἰοῦσα ἰόν.

37. The verb οἶδα 'know' is an old perfect with some archaic features. The stem is Ϝιδ- / Ϝειδ- / Ϝοιδ- (Lat. uideo, Eng. wit). Ind. sg. 1 οἶδα, 2 οἶσθα (< *Ϝοιδ·θα, -θα being an old perfect sg. 2 ending), 3 οἶδε; pl. 1 ἴσμεν (< *Ϝιδμεν), 2 ἴστε (< *Ϝιδτε), 3 ἴσᾱσι (for *Ϝιδντι). Ind. plu. sg. ᾔδη ᾔδησθα ᾔδει, pl. ᾖσμεν ᾖστε ᾖσαν. Sub. εἰδῶ, opt. εἰδείην, imp. ἴσθι ἴστω ἴστε ἴστων, inf. εἰδέναι, ptc. εἰδώς εἰδυῖα εἰδός.

38. Many verbs (mostly derived from nouns and hence called denominative verbs) end the stem in a vowel -α -ε or -ο which merges with the theme-vowel according to the laws of vowel contraction (Table IV C): τιμάω > τιμῶ 'honour', φιλέω > φιλῶ 'love', δηλόω > δηλῶ 'make clear' (from τιμά φίλος δῆλος). All the contracted forms can be deduced from Table IV C. The verbs belong to the type λύω, except for two features: (1) the optative singular active follows φαίην, not λύοιμι (τιμῴην φιλοίην δηλοίην); and (2) the infinitive is formed from -εν, not -ειν (τιμᾶν φιλεῖν δηλοῦν): see Table X. Contraction takes place only in the present and imperfect (active and medio-passive). The other tenses are formed by lengthening the stem vowel and follow λύω: fut τιμήσω φιλήσω δηλώσω, aor. ἐτίμησα ἐφίλησα ἐδήλωσα, per. τετίμηκα πεφίληκα δεδήλωκα.

39. The dual endings are: (1) primary: active 2-3 -ε·τον, medio-passive -ε·σθον, (2) secondary: active 2 -ε·τον 3 -έ·την, medio-passive 2 -ε·σθον 3 -έ·σθην, (3) imperative: active 2 -έ·τον 3 -έ·των, medio-passive -έ·σθω 3 -έ·σθων.

TABLE X

THE VERB: INFINITIVES AND PARTICIPLES

	Infinitives		Participles	
	active	medio-passive	active	medio-passive
1 pre.ᵃ	φάμεν φάναι	φάσθαι	φάς φᾶσα φάν	φάμεν-ος -η -ον
2 pre.ᵗ	λύειν	λύεσθαι	λύ-ων -ουσα -ον	λυόμεν-ος -η -ον
3 fut.	λύσειν	λύσεσθαι	λύσ-ων -ουσα -ον	λυσόμεν-ος -η -ον m λυθησόμεν-ος -η -ον p
4 aor.ᵃ	φάμεν φάναι	φάσθαι	φάς φᾶσα φάν	φάμεν-ος -η -ον
5 aor.ᵖ	φαθῆμεν φαθῆναι		φα-θείς -θεῖσα -θέν	
6 aor.ᵗ	λιπεῖν	λιπέσθαι	λιπ-ών -οῦσα -όν	λιπόμεν-ος -η -ον
7 aor.ˢ	λῦσαι	λύσασθαι	λύσ-ᾰς -ᾱσα -αν	λυσάμεν-ος -η -ον
8 per.	λελυκέναι	λελύσθαι	λελυκ-ώς -υῖα -ός	λελυμέν-ος -η -ον

Notes.

1. The infinitive endings are in origin dative case-endings, but their precise origin is obscure.
2. Inf. pre. aor.ᵃ act. Ep. φά·μεν, Att. φά·ναι: Ep. also φά·μεναι, which may be a combination of the two.
3. Inf. pre.ᵗ act. λύειν < λύ·ε·εν: -εν in contracted presents (Table IX.38).
4. φάς φᾶσα φάν, acc. φάντα φᾶσαν φάν, like πᾶς πᾶσα πᾶν (Table VII).
5. λύ·ων λύ·ουσα λύ·ον, gen. λύ-οντος -ούσης -οντος (λύουσα < *λυοντya).
6. φαθείς φαθεῖσα φαθέν, gen. φαθ-έντος -είσης -έντος (φαθεῖσα < *φαθεντya).
7. λύσ·ας λύ·σ·ασα λῦ·σ·αν like πᾶς πᾶσα πᾶν.
8. λε·λυ·κ·ώς λε·λυ·κ·υῖα λε·λυ·κ·ός, gen. λελυκ-ότος -υίας -ότος.
9. In addition to the participles, the AG verb had two verbal adjectives, which differ from the participles in not being inflected according to voice and tense: (1) φατ-ός -ή -όν 'said', λυτ-ός -ή -όν 'loosed' (negative

ἄφατ-ος -ον 'unsaid', ἄλυτ-ος -ον 'unloosed'; (2) φατέ-ος -α -ον λυτέ-ος -α -ον 'needing to be said' or 'loosed': τιμωρητέοι εἰσὶν οἱ ἀδικοῦντες 'offenders must be punished'. The second type was used in the neuter, with or without ἐστίν, in an impersonal sense: θεραπευτέον (ἐστὶ) τοὺς θεούς 'one must serve the gods'.

TABLE XI
THE VERB: REDUPLICATED ATHEMATIC STEMS

δί·δω·μι (δο-/δω-) 'give',   ἵ·στη·μι (στα/στη) 'stand',   τί·θη·μι (θε/θη) 'put'

Active

1	Pre. ind.	δίδωμι	δίδως	δίδωσι	δίδομεν	δίδοτε	διδόᾱσι
2		ἵστημι	ἵστης	ἵστησι	ἵσταμεν	ἵστατε	ἱστᾶσι
3		τίθημι	τίθης	τίθησι	τίθεμεν	τίθετε	τιθέᾱσι
4	Impf.	ἐδίδουν	ἐδίδους	ἐδίδου	ἐδίδομεν	ἐδίδοτε	ἐδίδοσαν
5		ἵστην	ἵστης	ἵστη	ἵσταμεν	ἵστατε	ἵστασαν
6		ἐτίθην	ἐτίθεις	ἐτίθει	ἐτίθεμεν	ἐτίθετε	ἐτίθεσαν
7	Pre. imp.		δίδου	διδότω		δίδοτε	διδόντων
8			ἵστη	ἱστάτω		ἵστατε	ἱστάντων
9			τίθει	τιθέτω		τίθετε	τιθέντων

| 10 | Pre. sub. | διδῶ | ἱστῶ | τιθῶ | Pre. opt. | διδοίην | ἱσταίην | τιθείην |
| 11 | Pre. inf. | διδόναι | ἱστάναι | τιθέναι | Pre. ptc. | διδούς | ἱστάς | τιθείς |

12	Aor. ind.	ἔδωκα	ἔδωκας	ἔδωκε	ἔδομεν	ἔδοτε	ἔδοσαν
13		ἔστην	ἔστης	ἔστη	ἔστημεν	ἔστητε	ἔστησαν
14		ἔθηκα	ἔθηκας	ἔθηκε	ἔθεμεν	ἔθετε	ἔθεσαν
15	Aor. imp		δός	δότω		δότε	δόντων
16			στῆθι	στήτω		στῆτε	στάντων
17			θές	θέτω		θέτε	θέντων

18	Aor. sub.	δῶ	στῶ	θῶ	Aor. opt.	δοίην	σταίην	θείην
19	Aor. inf.	δοῦναι	στῆναι	θεῖναι	Aor. ptc.	δούς	στάς	θείς
20	Fut. ind.	δώσω	στήσω	θήσω	Per. ind.	δέδωκα	ἕστηκα	τέθηκα

TABLE XI   THE VERB: REDUPLICATED ATHEMATIC STEMS   83

Medio-passive

1	Pre. ind.	δίδομαι	ἵσταμαι	τίθεμαι
2	Impf.	ἐδιδόμην	ἱστάμην	ἐτιθέμην
3	Pre. sub.	διδῶμαι	ἱστῶμαι	τιθῶμαι
4	Pre. opt.	διδοίμην	ἱσταίμην	τιθείμην
5	Pre. inf.	δίδοσθαι	ἵστασθαι	τίθεσθαι
6	Pre. ptc.	διδόμενος	ἱστάμενος	τιθέμενος
7	Pre. imp.	δίδοσο	ἵστασο	τίθεσο
8	Aor.ᵐ ind.	ἐδόμην	—	ἐθέμην
9	Aor.ᵐ imp.	δοῦ	—	θοῦ
10	Aor.ᵐ sub.	δῶμαι	—	θῶμαι
11	Aor.ᵐ opt.	δοίμην	—	θείμην
12	Aor.ᵐ inf.	δόσθαι	—	θέσθαι
13	Aor.ᵐ ptc.	δόμενος	—	θέμενος
14	Fut.ᵐ ind.	δώσομαι	στήσομαι	θήσομαι
15	Per. ind.	δέδομαι	—	—
16	Aor.ᵖ ind.	ἐδόθην	ἐστάθην	ἐτέθην
17	Fut.ᵖ ind.	δοθήσομαι	σταθήσομαι	τεθήσομαι

Notes.

1. ἵ·στη·μι < *σι·στᾱ·μι, τί·θη·μι < *θι·θη·μι.
2. Pre. ind. sg. 2 δίδως ἵστης τίθης with the secondary ending -ς in place of δίδωσι ἵστησι τίθησι: 3 δίδωσι ἵστησι τίθησι for ἵστᾱτι τίθητι δίδωτι by assibilation (XI.3.11). Pl. 3 διδόᾱσι for δίδοντι, ἱστᾶσι (< *ἱσταᾱσι) for ἵσταντι, τιθέᾱσι for τίθεντι: for the ending -ᾱσι see Table IX.25.
3. Impf. ἐδίδ-ουν -ους -ου (for ἐδιδ-ων -ως -ω), ἐτίθ-εις -ει (for ἐτιθ-ης -η): these forms have been influenced by thematic verbs of the types δηλῶ (-όω) and φιλῶ (-έω), which give ἐδήλ-ουν -ους -ου, ἐφίλ-εις -ει.
4. Pre. imp. sg. 2 δίδου τίθει for *διδο *τιθε on the analogy of δήλου φίλει.
5. Aor. ind. sg. ἔδω-κα -κας -κε ἔθη-κα -κας -κε for ἔδων *ἔθην etc. with -κα -κες -κε borrowed from the perfect: HG gives also ἐδώκαμεν ἐθή-καμεν etc. Pl. 3 ἔδοσαν etc. for ἔδον etc. < *ἔδοντ.
6. Aor. imp. sg. 2 δό·ς θέ·ς with the secondary sg. 2 ending -ς.
7. Aor. mid. sg. 2 ἔδου ἔθου < *ἐδοσο *ἐθεσο.
8. Aor. mid. imp. sg. 2 δοῦ θοῦ < *δοσο *θεσο.
9. Aor.ᵖ ind. ἐτέθην < *ἐ·θε·θη·ν: XI.3.15.
10. Sub. διδῶ and δῶ retain the ῶ (ῷ) throughout.

TABLE XII

THE VERB: PARADIGMS

Pre.	Fut.	Aor.	Aor.ᴾ	Peɾ.	
1 ἄγω lead	ἄξω	ἤγαγον	ἤχθην	ἦγμαι	ἀγωγή f. lead
2 αἰσθάνομαι perceive	αἰσθήσομαι	ᾐσθόμην		ᾔσθημαι	αἴσθησις f. feeling
3 ἀκούω hear	ἀκούσομαι	ἤκουσα	ἠκούσθην	ἀκήκοα	ἀκοή f. hearing
4 ἀποθνῄσκω die	ἀποθανοῦμαι	ἀπέθανον		τέθνηκα	θάνατος m. death
5 ἀφικνοῦμαι arrive	ἀφίξομαι	ἀφικόμην		ἀφῖγμαι	ἄφιξις f. arrival
6 βάλλω throw	βαλῶ (-έω)	ἔβαλον	βέβληκα	βέβλημαι	βολή f. throw
7 γίγνομαι become	γενήσομαι	ἐγενόμην		γέγονα γεγένημαι	γένεσις f. birth
8 ἐγείρω awake tr.	ἐγερῶ (-έω)	ἤγειρα	ἠγέρθην	ἐγρήγορα	ἔγερσις f. awakening
9 ἔρχομαι come, go	ἐλεύσομαι	ἦλθον (ἐλθ-)		ἐλήλυθα	
10 εὑρίσκω find	εὑρήσω	ηὗρον	ηὑρέθην	ηὕρηκα ηὕρημαι	εὕρημα n. discovery
11 ἔχω have, hold	ἕξω σχήσω	ἔσχον	ἐσχέθην	ἔσχηκα	ὀχεύς m. fastener
12 θαυμάζω wonder	θαυμάσομαι	ἐθαύμασα	ἐθαυμάσθην	τεθαύμακα	θαῦμα n. wonder
13 μένω stay	μενῶ (-έω)	ἔμεινα		μεμένηκα	μονή f. delay
14 πάσχω suffer	πείσομαι	ἔπαθον		πέπονθα	πάθος n. plight
15 πείθω persuade	πείσω	ἔπιθον ἔπεισα	ἐπείσθην	πέποιθα πέπεισμαι	πειθώ f. persuasion
16 πήγνυμι fix	πήξω	ἔπηξα	ἐπάγην ἐπήχθην	πέπηγα πέπηγμαι	παγή f. frost
17 σῴζω save	σώσω	ἔσωσα	ἐσώθην	σέσω(σ)μαι	σωτήρ (-ηρ-) m. saviour

TABLE XII   THE VERB: PARADIGMS   85

Pre.	Fut.	Aor.	Aor.ᵖ	Per.	
τρέφω nourish	θρέψω	ἔτραφον ἔθρεψα	ἐτράφην ἐθρέφθην	τέτροφα τέθραμμαι	τροφή f. nurture
τυγχάνω happen	τεύξομαι	ἔτυχον		τετύχηκα	τύχη f. chance
φαίνω show	φανῶ (-έω)	ἔφηνα	ἐφάνην ἐφάνθην	πέφηνα πέφασμαι	φανερ-ός -ά -όν manifest
φέρω bear	οἴσω	ἤνεγκα ἤνεγκον	ἠνέχθην	ἐνήνοχα	φόρος m. tax
φροντίζω care	φροντιῶ (-έω)	ἐφρόντισα		πεφρόντικα	φροντίς (-ίδ-) f. care
ψεύδω deceive	ψεύσω	ἔψευσα	ἐψεύσθην	ἔψευσμαι	ψεῦδος n. lie

Notes.

Present.

1. In many verbs the present stem was formed from the simple stem (commonly preserved in the aorist) by means of infixes, which were originally marks of aspect: -αν- (αἰσθάνομαι, τυγχάνω), -σκ- (ἀπο-θνήσκω), πάσχω < *πνθ·σκ·ω), -νε- (ἀφικνοῦμαι < ἀφ·ικ·νέ·ομαι), -y-(βάλλω < *βαλ·y·ω, ἐγείρω < *ἐγερ·y·ω, φαίνω < *φαν·y·ω, φροντίζω < *φροντιδ·y·ω), -νυ- (πήγνυμι).

2. The present τυγχάνω, formed from the stem τυχ- with a radical infix -ν- as well as the post-radical infix -αν-, belongs to a large class of verbs: μανθάνω (μαθ-) 'learn', λαμβάνω (λαβ-) 'take', λανθάνω (λαθ-) 'be hidden', χανδάνω (χαδ-) 'contain', ἀνδάνω (ἀδ-) 'please', κιγχάνω (κιχ-) 'go', etc.

3. Some presents are formed by reduplication: γίγνομαι (γεν-), μίμνω (μεν-) 'remain', πίμπλημι (πλη-) 'fill'. πίμπρημι (πρη-) 'burn', γιγνώσκω (γνω-) 'recognise', etc. There are also a few verbs in which it is the aorist stem that is reduplicated: ἄγω ἤγαγον.

4. The present εὑρίσκω is formed with the infix -ισκ-, an extended form of -σκ- which was created on the analogy of such verbs as ἀρ·αρί·σκω (root αρι-, cf. ἀριθμός 'number') 'fit': so ἁλίσκομαι 'be caught', στερίσκω 'rob'; hence the spellings θνήσκω μιμνήσκω etc. for θνήσκω μιμνήσκω. The infix -ζ- (< -δy)- was extended in the same way to -ιζ- -αζ-: ἀνδρίζω 'be a man', εὐδαιμονίζω 'congratulate', καλλωπίζω 'beautify'; also σώζω > σῴζω; θαυμάζω, ἡσυχάζω etc.

Future.

5. The future infix -σ- is also found in the extended forms -εσ- and -ησ-, the former being subject to loss of intervocalic -σ-: ἀποθανοῦμαι < *ἀποθανεσομαι), βαλῶ (< *βαλεσω), ἐγερῶ, μενῶ, φανῶ, φροντιῶ etc.

6. Many active presents have a middle future: ἀκούσομαι, θαυμάσομαι, πείσομαι, τεύξομαι. Being in origin a subjective or volitional future, this tense had tended to be most commonly used in the middle voice.

Augment.

7. Verb stems beginning with a consonant take the augment without change: βάλλω ἔβαλλον ἔβαλον, γίγνομαι ἐγιγνόμην ἐγενόμην. Where the stem begins with a vowel, the augment was formed by lengthening it: ἰκνοῦμαι ἰκνούμην ἰκόμην, ἐγείρω ἤγειρον ἤγειρα, ἔρχομαι ἠρχόμην ἦλθον (ἐλθ-). These forms are perhaps due to the analogy of ἦ 'I was' < ἦα < IE *ēs·m̥ *e·es·m̥ (see Table XIII). In a few verbs we find ἠ- (possibly an IE by-form) for ἐ-, which with the following vowel suffers quantitative metathesis (XI.3.14): ὁρῶ (-άω) ἑώρων.

8. Verbs compounded with a preposition normally take the augment after the preposition: ἀποθνῄσκω ἀπέθνῃσκον ἀπέθανον, ἀφικνοῦμαι ἀφικνούμην ἀφικόμην.

Aorist.

9. For the reduplicated aorist ἤγαγον see above 3.

10. The aor. ἔφηνα stands for *εφανσα: XI.3.16.

11. ἔχω ἔσχον: PG *σεχ·ω *σεχ·σω ἔ·σχον *σε·σχη·κα. The initial σ- became a breathing (XI.3.7), which was lost (XI.3.15), except in the future, where the following χ was deaspirated.

12. πάσχω ἔπαθον: see XI.4.

Perfect.

13. Stems in ψ- σπ- στ- reduplicate with ἐ- on the analogy of the augment: ψεύδω ἔψευσμαι, σπείρω ἔσπαρκα, στέλλω ἔσταλκα.

TABLE XIII
THE VERB 'TO BE'

	IE	AG					MG
		Doric	Epic	Ionic	Attic	HG	
Pre.	*es·mi	εἰμί	εἰμί	εἰμί	εἰμί	εἰμί	εἶμαι
	*es-si	ἐσσί	ἐσσί εἶς	εἶς	εἶ	εἶ	εἶσαι
	*es·ti	ἐστί	ἐστί	ἐστί	ἐστί	ἐστί ἔνι	εἶναι
	*s·mes	εἰμές	εἰμέν	εἰμέν	ἐσμέν	ἐσμέν	εἴμαστε
	*s·te	ἐστέ	ἐστέ	ἐστέ	ἐστέ	ἐστέ	εἶστε
	*s·e·nti	ἐντί	εἰσί ἔᾱσι	εἰσί	εἰσί	εἰσί ἔνι	εἶναι
Impf.	*ēs·m	ἦν	ἦα	ἦα ἔᾱ	ἦ ἦν	ἦν ἤμην	ἤμουν
	*ēs·s	ἦσθα	ἦσθα	ἦσθα ἔᾱς	ἦσθα	ἦς ἦσο	ἤσουν
	*ēs·t	ἦς	ἦεν	ἦν	ἦν	ἦν ἦτο	ἦτο ἦταν
	*ēs·me	ἦμες	ἦμεν	ἦμεν	ἦσμεν ἦμεν	ἦμεν	ἤμαστε
	*ēs·te	ἦστε	ἦτε	ἦτε	ἦστε ἦτε	ἦτε	ἤσαστε
	*ēs·e·nt	ἦν	ἦσαν	ἦσαν	ἦσαν	ἦσαν	ἦσαν ἦταν

Notes.

1. AG. Present. Sg. 1 Aeo. ἐμμί. Sg. 2 Ep. Ion. εἶς after λύεις; Att. εἶ < *ἐσί. Pl. 1 Att. ἐσμέν for εἰμέν after ἐστέ. Pl. 3 Ep. ἔᾱσι cf. τιθέᾱσι (Table XI.3). Sg. pl. 3 HG ἔνι for ἔνεστι ἔνεισι. Imperfect. Sg. 1 Dor. Att. ἦν for ἦ after ἔφην; Ep. Ion. ἦα < * ἦσα; Ion. ἔᾱ: XI.3.14. Sg. 2 ἦσθα: Table IX.5. HG ἤμην ἦσο ἦτο middle after fut. ἔσομαι. Sg. 3 Ion. Att. ἦν originally pl. 3, as in Doric. Pl. 3 ἦσαν after ἔφασαν.

2. MG. Present. Sg. 1 εἶμαι middle after ἤμην, so sg. 2 εἶσαι. Sg. pl. 3 εἶναι for HG ἔνι after εἶμαι εἶσαι. Pl. 1-2 εἴμαστε εἶστε < εἴμεθα εἶσθε. Imperfect. Sg. 1 ἤμουν for HG ἤμην after ἤσουν. Sg. 2 ἤσουν for ἦσο with -ν after ἦταν. Sg. 3 ἦταν for ἦτο with -αν after ἦσαν. Pl. 1-2 ἤμαστε ἤσαστε for ἤμεθα ἦσθε. Pl. 3 ἦταν for ἦσαν after ἦτο, with a common form for sg. and pl. as in the present (εἶναι). The ending -ταν was extended by analogy from ἦταν to the impf. mp. sg. pl. 3 of the regular verb: see Table XVI.

3. It will be seen that, while the MG forms can all be accounted for, they have been subjected to so many analogical changes that the AG forms, if they had not survived in written records, would have been irrecoverable.

4. For the other parts of AG εἰμί see Table IX.35.

TABLE XIV

' WORD-FORMATION

The words at the head of each group are taken from Tables VI, VII and XII.

1 παῖς child; παίζω play; παιδεύω educate; παιδευτής educator; παιδευτήριον school; παῖγμα sport; παιδιά pastime; παιδεία training; παιδίον παιδάριον παιδίσκος child; παιδικός pertaining to children; παιδαγωγός tutor; παιδοποιός childbearing; παιδοποιῶ (-έω) bear children; ἄπαις childless; ἀπαίδευτος uneducated; εὔπαις having good or many children; εὐπαίδευτος well-educated. (MG παιδί).

2 φύλαξ guard; φυλάττω guard; φυλακή guard, watch; φυλακτήριον fort; προφυλακή outpost; προφυλάττομαι take precautions; ἀφύλακτος unguarded. (MG φύλακας).

3 ῥήτωρ speaker; ῥῆσις speech; ῥῆμα word; ἀπόρρητος secret; ἄρρητος unspeakable; παρρησία freedom of speech; ῥητορική rhetoric. (MG ῥήτορας).

4 δαίμων god; δαιμόνιος miraculous; δαιμονῶ (-άω) δαιμονίζομαι be possessed; εὐδαίμων happy; εὐδαιμονία bliss; εὐδαιμονῶ (-έω) be happy; δυσδαίμων unhappy; δυσδαιμονία, δυσδαιμονῶ (-έω); δεισιδαίμων superstitious, δεισιδαιμονία. (MG δαίμονας).

5 λέων lion; λεόντειος λεοντικός of a lion; λεοντεία ferocity; λεοντώδης lionlike; λέαινα lioness. (MG λιοντάρι).

6 σῶμα body; σωματικός bodily; σωματοφύλαξ bodyguard; σωματῶ (-όω) embody; ἀσώματος incorporeal. (MG σῶμα).

7 ἱερός holy; ἱερεύς priest; ἱέρεια priestess; ἱερεία sacrifice; ἱερεῖον victim; ἱερῶ (-όω) sanctify; ἱερεύω sacrifice; ἱερωσύνη sanctity; ἀνίερος unholy. (MG ἱερός).

8 Σωκράτης Socrates; Σωκρατικός Socratic; σωκρατῶ (-έω) σωκρατίζω behave like Socrates; σωκρατιστής imitator of S.

9 γένος race, kin; γενικός general; γένεσις birth; εὐγενής well-born; εὐγένεια nobility; δυσγενής baseborn; δυσγένεια ignobility; συγγενής kinsman; συγγένεια kinship. (MG γένος).

10 αἰδώς shame; αἰδοῖος awe-inspiring, bashful; ἀναιδής shameless; ἀναίδεια shamelessness; αἰδοῦμαι (-εο-) be ashamed.

TABLE XIV WORD-FORMATION 89

11 πατήρ father; πάτριος πατρικός πατρῷος paternal; πάτρως father's brother; πατροῦχος heiress; ἀπάτωρ fatherless; φιλοπάτωρ loving one's father; πάτρα πατρίς fatherland; πατριώτης fellow-countryman; πατροπαράδοτος inherited from father to son. (MG πατέρας).

12 ἀνήρ man; ἀνδρεῖος brave; ἀνδρεία bravery; ἀνδρότης manhood; ἀνδρικός manly; ἀνδρίζω make a man of; ἀνδρών men's quarters; πολύανδρος populous. (MG ἄντρας).

13 ἰχθύς fish; ἰχθύα fishing; ἰχθυῶ (-άω) fish; ἰχθυηρός fishy; ἰχθυοειδής fish-like.

14 πῆχυς forearm; πήχυιος πηχυαῖος one cubit long; πηχύνω take into one's arms. (MG πήχη).

15 πόλις city; πολίτης citizen; πολιτεύω be a citizen; πολιτικός political; πολιτεία republic; ἄπολις cityless; φιλόπολις patriotic; πολίζω build a city; πόλισμα town; πολιορκῶ (-έω) besiege; πολιορκία siege. (MG πόλη).

16 ἄστυ town; ἀστικός urban; ἀστεῖος urbane, witty; ἀστειότης refinement; ἀστυνόμος chief of police; προάστιον suburb. (MG ἀστεῖος).

17 λόγος saying; λέγω say; λέξις speech; ἄλογος speechless; πολύλογος verbose; φιλόλογος fond of learning; φιλολογία love of learning; λόγιος learned; λόγιμος notable; εὔλογος eloquent; κακόλογος evil-speaking; διάλογος conversation; διαλέγομαι discuss; λογίζομαι reckon; λογισμός reasoning. (MG λόγος).

18 νεώς temple; νεωκόρος sacristan; νεωποιός temple maintenance officer. (MG ναός).

19 πλοῖον boat; πλέω sail; πλοῦς (< πλόος) voyage; εὔπλοια good voyage; εὐπλοῶ (-έω) have a good voyage; ἄπλους unseaworthy. (MG πλοῖο).

20 ὥρα season; ὡραῖος seasonable; ὡραιότης ripeness; ὡραΐζω beautify; ἔνωρος early; ἄωρος unripe; πρόωρος premature. (MG ὥρα).

21 λύπη grief; λυπῶ (-έω) grieve; ἄλυπος without grief; λυπηρός grievous. (MG λύπη).

22 σφαῖρα ball; σφαιρῶ (-έω) make into a ball; σφαιρικός spherical; σφαίριστρα σφαιριστήριον ball-court. (MG σφαῖρα).

23 χλαῖνα cloak; χλαινῶ (-όω) cover with a cloak; χλαινηφόρος wearing a cloak. (MG χλαῖνα).

24 ταμίας steward; ταμιεία stewardship; ταμιεῖον storehouse; ταμιεύω be paymaster, dispense. (MG ταμίας).

25 ναύτης sailor; ναῦς ship; ναυτικός nautical; ναυτίλος seaman; ναυτεία seamanship; ναυτία seasickness; ναυτιῶ (-άω) be seasick; ναυαγῶ (-έω) suffer shipwreck; ναυαγία shipwreck; ναυαρχῶ (-έω) command a fleet; ναύαρχος admiral; ναυπηγεῖον shipyard. (MG ναύτης).

26 πᾶς all; παντοῖος of all sorts; παντοδαπός from all countries; πανταχοῦ everywhere; πάντοτε at all times; πάντοσε in all directions; πάντοθεν from all directions; παντάπασι entirely; πάντως at any rate; πάγκαλος very fine; παγκράτιον all-in wrestling; παγκρατής all-powerful; παντόπτης all-seeing. (MG πάντα always).

27 ἄφρων foolish; φρήν midriff, φρένες pl. sense; ἀφρονῶ (-έω) be foolish; ἀφροσύνη folly; σώφρων wise, σωφρονῶ (-έω), σωφροσύνη; εὔφρων merry, εὐφρονῶ (-έω), εὐφροσύνη. (MG ἄφρων).

28 βαρύς heavy; βάρος n. weight; βαρύτης f. heaviness; βαρύνω weigh down, oppress; βαρύτονος deep (of voice); θυμοβαρής heavy-hearted. (MG βαρύς).

29 σαφής clear; ἀσαφής obscure; ἀσάφεια obscurity; σαφηνίζω clarify; σαφήνεια clarity. (MG σαφηνίζω).

30 μέλας black; τὸ μέλαν ink; μελαίνω blacken; μελανία blackness; μελαγχολία melancholy; μελάνυδρος with black water. (MG τὸ μελάνι ink).

31 σοφός wise; σοφία wisdom; σοφίζομαι contrive; σόφισμα device; σοφιστής wise man; φιλόσοφος philosopher; φιλοσοφῶ (-έω) practise philosophy; φιλοσοφία philosophy. (MG σοφός).

32 ἄγω lead; ἀγωγή freight, guidance, training; ἀγώγιμος portable, easily led; εὐαγωγός docile; ἐπαγωγός attractive; εἰσαγωγή import; ἐξαγωγή export. (MG ἀγωγή).

33 αἰσθάνομαι feel; αἴσθησις sensation; αἴσθημα feeling; ἀναίσθητος insensible; αἰσθητήριον sense-organ. (MG αἰσθάνομαι).

34 ἀφικνοῦμαι, ἱκνοῦμαι come; ἄφιξις arrival; ἐφικτός accessible.

35 ἀκούω hear: ἀκοή hearing; ἀκουστής hearer; ἄκουσμα sound; ἀκουστήριον lecture-hall; ἀνήκουστος inaudible, unheard of; ἀνηκουστῶ (-έω) disobey. (MG ἀκούω).

TABLE XIV   WORD-FORMATION   91

36 ἀποθνήσκω, θνήσκω die; θάνατος death; θνητός mortal; ἀθάνατος immortal; θανάσιμος deadly; θανατηφόρος death-dealing; θανατῶ (-όω) put to death; θανατῶ (-άω) long to die, be moribund. (MG πεθαίνω, aor. πέθανα).

37 βάλλω throw; βολή a throw; βέλος n. weapon; βόλος net; βελόνη needle; βλῆμα a throw (of dice); βλητρίζω toss. (MG βάλλω).

38 γίγνομαι be born, become; γένος kin, kind; γένεσις birth; γόνος offspring; γόνιμος fertile; ἀπόγονος ἔκγονος descendant; ἐπίγονος successor; πρόγονος ancestor; σύγγονος kin; ἄγονος childless; πολύγονος prolific; γνήσιος genuine. (MG γίνομαι).

39 ἐγείρω wake; ἔγερσις awakening; ἐγερτικός rousing; ἐγρηγορικός waking. (MG γρήγορος).

40 εὑρίσκω find: εὑρετής discoverer; εὕρεσις discovery; εὕρημα a discovery; εὑρησίλογος resourceful in argument; δυσεύρετος hard to find; ἀνεύρετος undiscovered. (MG βρίσκω).

41 ἔχω hold; ὀχυρός firm, ὀχυρῶ (-όω) fortify; ὀχμάζω grip; ἕξις condition; σχῆμα shape; σχηματίζω gesticulate, fashion; ἄσχετος ungovernable. (MG ἔχω).

42 θαυμάζω wonder; θαῦμα wonder; θαυμάσιος wonderful; θαυματοποιία conjuring; θαυματουργῶ (-έω) work miracles. (MG θαυμάζω).

43 πάσχω suffer; πάθος n. experience; πάθημα misfortune; ἀπαθής insensible, ἀπάθεια apathy; εὐπαθής luxurious, εὐπάθεια comfort; εὐπαθῶ (-έω) enjoy oneself. (MG παθαίνω).

44 πείθω persuade; πειθώ persuasion; εὐπειθής obedient, εὐπείθεια; ἀπειθής disobedient, ἀπείθεια; δυσπειθής refractory, δυσπείθεια indiscipline; πιθανός persuasive, plausible. (MG πείθω).

45 πήγνυμι fasten, fix; πάγη παγίς snare; πάγιος firm; πάγος παγετός frost; ναυπηγός shipwright; ναυπηγεῖον shipyard. (MG πήζω curdle).

46 σῴζω save; σωτήρ saviour; σωτηρία salvation; σώφρων wise, σωφροσύνη wisdom, σωφρονῶ (-έω) be wise, sensible; ἄσωτος desperate, abandoned; ἀσωτία profligacy. (MG σώνω).

47 τρέφω feed, rear; τροφή nourishment; τροφός nurse; τροφεῖα (n. pl.) pay for maintenance; τροφεύς foster-father; τρόφιμος nutritious; ἄτροφος ill-fed; ἀτροφία malnutrition, atrophy; εὐτραφής thriving. (MG θρέφω).

48 τυγχάνω hit, happen; τύχη chance; εὐτυχής lucky, εὐτυχία good luck, εὐτύχημα piece of luck, εὐτυχῶ (-έω) be lucky; δυστυχής, δυστυχία, δυστύχημα, δυστυχῶ (-έω); ἀτυχής, ἀτυχία, ἀτύχημα, ἀτυχῶ (-έω); τυχηρός lucky. (MG τυχαίνω).

---

49 φαίνω show; φάσμα apparition; ἄφαντος vanished; φανερός visible, φανερῶ (-όω) make manifest; φαντάζομαι become visible; φαντασία appearance, imagination. (MG φαίνομαι).

---

50 φέρω bear; φορά motion; φόρος tribute; φόρτος freight, φορτίζω to load; φορτηγός merchant; φορεύς bearer; φορῶ (-έω) bear, wear, φόρημα load; φόριμος fruit-bearing; φορμός basket, mat; ἄφορος barren; εὔφορος fertile, vigorous, εὐφορῶ (-έω), εὐφορία. (MG φέρνω).

---

51 φροντίζω, φροντίς care; ἀφρόντιστος heedless; ἄφροντις carefree. (MG φροντίζω).

---

52 ψεύδω deceive; ψεῦδος n. ψεῦσμα ψῦθος n. lie; ψευδής false; ἀψευδής infallible; ψευδομαρτυρία false witness; ψευδώνυμος miscalled. (MG ψέμα).

TABLE XV

PREPOSITIONS

1 ἀμφί (acc.) ἀμφὶ τὴν πόλιν around the city; ἀμφὶ τὸ δεῖπνον about supper-time; οἱ ἀμφὶ Σωκράτη the followers of Socrates; (in composition) ἀμφιβάλλω put round (clothes); ἀμφίβολος doubtful; ἀμπέχω put on (clothes).

---

2 ἀνά (acc.) ἀνὰ τὸν ποταμόν up the river; ἀνὰ τὸν πόλεμον throughout the war; (in composition) ἀνάγω lead up, lift; ἀναβάλλω throw up, defer; ἀνεγείρω wake up (tr.); ἀνέρχομαι ascend; ἀνευρίσκω discover; ἀνέχω hold up; ἀναμένω await; ἀναπείθω convince, mislead; ἀναπήγνυμι impale; ἀνασῴζω recover, rescue; ἀνατρέφω feed up; ἀναφαίνω show up, proclaim; ἀναφέρω carry up, carry back, refer; ἀναφροντίζω ponder over.

---

3 ἀντί (gen.) ἀντὶ λόγων ἔργα deeds instead of words; ἀντακούω hear in turn; ἀντιβάλλω throw against, compare; ἀντιβολῶ (-έω) confront; ἀντέχω withstand; ἀντιπάσχω suffer in return; ἀντιτυγχάνω encounter; ἀντιφέρομαι pit oneself against.

TABLE XV   PREPOSITIONS   93

4 ἀπό (gen.) ἀπ' οἴκου away from home; ἀπὸ τούτου τοῦ χρόνου from that time; ἀπὸ τύχης by accident; (in composition) ἀπάγω arrest; ἀποβάλλω throw away, lose; ἀπογίγνομαι be absent; ἀπέρχομαι depart; ἀπέχω hold off, be far from; ἀποπήγνυμαι freeze up; ἀποσῴζω rescue; ἀποτρέφομαι feed on; ἀποτυγχάνω miss, fail; ἀποφαίνω show off, denounce; ἀποφέρω carry off, bring back, repay.

5 διά (acc.) διὰ δώματα through the rooms; διὰ νύκτα through the night; διὰ ταῦτα for that reason, that is why; (gen.) ἔφυγον διὰ τῆς πόλεως they fled through the city; διὰ νυκτός through the night; διὰ φόβου in a state of fear; (in composition) διάγω spend (time); διακούω hear to the end; διαβάλλω set at variance, slander; διαγίγνομαι elapse; διεγείρω excite; διέρχομαι pass through, elapse; διαμένω persevere; διαπήγνυμι transfix; διασῴζω preserve; διαφαίνομαι show through; διαφανής transparent; διαψεύδω cheat.

6 εἰς ἐς (acc.) εἰς τὴν πόλιν to the city; εἰς νύκτα till nightfall; (in composition) εἰσάγω introduce, import; εἰσακούω hearken to; εἰσβάλλω throw in, enter; εἰσέρχομαι enter.

7 ἐκ ἐξ (ἐξ before vowels) (gen.) ἐκ τῆς πόλεως out of the city; ἐκ τούτου from then; (in composition) ἐξάγω produce, export; ἐκβάλλω cast out; ἐκγίγνομαι be born of; ἐξεγείρω wake up (tr.); ἐξέρχομαι go out; ἐξευρίσκω find out; ἐξέχω stand out; ἔξοχος excellent.

8 ἐν (dat.) ἐν τῇ πόλει in the city; ἐν χρόνῳ in time; ἐν φόβῳ in fear; (in composition) ἐνάγω urge; ἐμβάλλω put in, break in; ἐγγίγνομαι be born in, be among; ἐμμένω abide, abide by; ἐνέχω be liable to.

9 ἐπί (acc.) ἐφ' ἵππον ἀναβαίνω mount a horse; ἐπὶ δύο ἡμέρας for two days; τὸ ἐπ' ἐμέ as far as I am concerned; (gen.) ἐπὶ νεῶν on shipboard; ἐφ' ἵππων on horseback; ἐπὶ Σωκράτους in Socrates' time; ἐφ' ἡμῶν in our time; (dat.) αἱ ἐπὶ θαλάττῃ πόλεις the cities on the sea; ἐπὶ τούτοις on these conditions; (in composition) ἐπάγω invite; ἐπακούω overhear; ἐπιβάλλω impose, assault; ἐπιγίγνομαι be born after, fall due; ἐπεγείρω wake up (tr.); ἐπέρχομαι come upon, attack; ἐπέχω offer, aim at, check, occupy; ἐπιμένω continue, endure; ἐπιπείθομαι comply with; ἐπιτυγχάνω attain, succeed; ἐπιφαίνω show forth; ἐπιφανής distinguished.

10 κατά (acc.) κατὰ τὸν ποταμόν down the river; κατ' ἐκεῖνον τὸν χρόνον at that time; κατὰ τοὺς νόμους according to the laws; (gen.) κατὰ

τῆς κλίμακος down the ladder; (in composition) κατάγω reduce; κατακούω obey; κατήκοος obedient; καταβάλλω drop, deposit; κατέρχομαι descend, return; κατέχω restrain, occupy; καταμένω stay; καταπήγνυμι plant firmly; καταφαίνομαι appear; καταφέρω demolish; καταψεύδομαι allege, pretend.

11 μετά (acc.) μετὰ ταῦτα after that; (gen.) μετὰ τῶν συμμάχων μάχεσθαι to fight with one's allies; (in composition) μεταβάλλω turn round, change; μετέρχομαι go among, migrate; μετέχω share; μεταφέρω transfer.

12 παρά (acc.) ἥκω παρὰ σέ I have come to you; παρὰ τὴν γῆν ἔπλει he sailed along the coast; παρὰ πάντα τὸν χρόνον during all the time; παρὰ τοὺς νόμους against the laws; (gen.) ἀφικνεῖται αὐτοῖς ἀγγελία παρὰ τῶν ἐπιτηδείων a message reaches them from their friends; (dat.) παρὰ σοί at your house; (in composition) παράγω lead past, mislead; παρακούω mishear, disregard: παρέρχομαι pass, outstrip; παρέχω provide; παραμένω stand by; παραπείθω win over, seduce; παρατρέφω bring up with; παραφαίνω expose.

13 περί (acc.) περὶ τὴν πόλιν around the town; περὶ δύο ἡμέρας for about two days; τὰ περὶ τὰς ναῦς naval affairs; (gen.) περὶ τοιούτων λέγειν to talk about such things; (in composition) περιάγω lead round, perplex; περιβάλλω put round, encompass; περιγίγνομαι surpass, survive; περιέρχομαι go round; περιέχω surround, surpass; περιμένω wait; περιφανής conspicuous; περιφέρω carry round; περιφερής revolving.

14 πρό (gen.) πρὸ τῆς πόλεως in front of the city; πρὸ τοῦ before this; πρὸ τούτου in preference to this; (in composition) προάγω induce; προαίσθησις presentiment; προακούω hear beforehand; προέρχομαι proceed; προεξέρχομαι go out first; προέχω hold forward, project; προφαίνω foreshow; προφέρω bring forward.

15 πρός (acc.) πρὸς τὴν πόλιν towards the city; πρὸς φυλακήν for protection; (gen.) πρὸς τοῦ ποταμοῦ near the river; (dat.) πρὸς τῇ πόλει near the city; πρὸς τούτοις in addition to this; (in composition) προσάγω put to, add; προσβάλλω strike, attack; προσγίγνομαι be added, accrue; προσέρχομαι approach; προσέχω attend; προσμένω await; προστυγχάνω obtain; προσφέρω apply.

TABLE XV   PREPOSITIONS   95

16 σύν ξύν (dat.) ἐπαιδεύετο σὺν τῷ ἀδελφῷ he was brought up with his brother; (in composition) συνάγω bring together; συμβάλλω put together, contribute; συγγίγνομαι consort with; συνέρχομαι come together; συνέχω hold together, secure; συμπάσχω feel with; συντρέφομαι grow up with; συμφέρω agree with, suit; συνασοφεῖν τοῖς μὴ σοφοῖς join with fools in folly.

17 ὑπέρ (acc.) ὑπὲρ τὴν θάλατταν beyond the sea; ὑπὲρ τὰ στρατεύσιμα ἔτη over military age; ὑπὲρ δύναμιν beyond one's power; (gen.) ὑπὲρ σοῦ on your behalf; (in composition) ὑπερβάλλω throw beyond, surpass; ὑπερέρχομαι pass over, cross; ὑπερέχω hold over, rise above.

18 ὑπό (acc.) ἀπῆλθον ὑπὸ τὰ δένδρα they went away under the trees; ὑπὸ νύκτα at nightfall; ὑπὸ βασιλέα under the King's rule; (gen.) ὑπὸ γῆς under the earth; πείθεσθαι ὑφ' ὑμῶν to be persuaded by you; (dat.) τί ἔχει ὑπὸ τῇ χλαίνῃ; what has he under his cloak? (in composition) ὑπάγω to subject, go; ὑπακούω answer (a call); ὑπήκοος subject; ὑποβάλλω put under, suggest; ὑπέρχομαι come under, steal upon; ὑπέχω support; ὑπομένω endure; ὑποτρέφω cherish.

TABLE XVI
THE MG NOUN AND VERB
A. *The Substantive*

		Sg.			Pl.		
N		V	A	G	NV	A	G
1 παιδί n.		〰〰	〰〰	παιδιοῦ	παιδιά	〰〰	παιδιῶν
2 φύλακας m.		φύλακα	φύλακα(ν)	φύλακα	φύλακες	〰〰	φυλάκων
3 σῶμα n.		〰〰	〰〰	σώματος	σώματα	〰〰	σωμάτων
4 γένος n.		〰〰	〰〰	γένους	γένη	〰〰	γενῶν
5 λόγος m.		λόγε	λόγο(ν)	λόγου	λόγοι	λόγους	λόγων
6 πλοῖο n.		〰〰	〰〰	πλοίου	πλοῖα	〰〰	πλοίων
7 ὥρα f.		〰〰	ὥρα(ν)	ὥρας	ὧρες	〰〰	ὡρῶν
8 λύπη f.		〰〰	λύπη(ν)	λύπης	λῦπες	〰〰	λυπῶν
9 ναύτης m.		ναύτη	ναύτη(ν)	ναύτη	ναῦτες	〰〰	ναυτῶν

8

B. *The Adjective*

1 σοφ-ός -ή -ό like λόγος λύπη πλοῖο.

2 βαρ-ύς -ιά -ύ	ᴧᴧᴧᴧ	-ύ -ιά -ύ	-ιοῦ -ιᾶς -ιοῦ	-ιοί -ιές -ιά	-ιούς -ιές -ιά	-ιῶν

3 Comparative: σοφώτερος or πιὸ σοφός, βαρύτερος or πιὸ βαρύς.

4 Superlative: ὁ σοφώτερος or ὁ πιὸ σοφός, ὁ βαρύτερος or ὁ πιὸ βαρύς.

C. *The Article, Definite and Indefinite*

1 ὁ ἡ τό	ᴧᴧᴧᴧ	τόν τή(ν) τό	τοῦ τῆς τοῦ	οἱ οἱ τά	τούς τές τά	τῶν
2 ἕνας μιά ἕνα	—	ἕνα(ν) μιά ἕνα	ἑνός μιᾶς ἑνός			

D. *The Personal Pronouns*

1 ἐγώ	—	μέ ἐμένα	μοῦ ἐμένα	ἐμεῖς	μᾶς ἐμᾶς	μᾶς
2 ἐσύ	—	σέ ἐσένα	σοῦ ἐσένα	ἐσεῖς	σᾶς ἐσᾶς	σᾶς
3 αὐτ-ός -ή -ό	—	τόν τή(ν) τό	τοῦ τῆς τοῦ	αὐτ-οί -ές -ά	τούς τές τά	τούς (των)

4 Relative ποὺ indeclinable. Reflexive τὸν ἑαυτό μου (σου, του, μας, σας, τους).

E. *The Verb*:

(1) λύνω loosen

1 Act. ind. pre.	λύνω	λύνεις	λύνει	λύνουμε	λύνετε	λύνουν
2 Act. ind. aor.	ἔλυσα	ἔλυσες	ἔλυσε	ἐλύσαμε	ἐλύσετε	ἔλυσαν

3 Act. ind. impf. ἔλυνα. Imp. pre. λῦνε λύνετε, aor. λῦσε λῦστε.

4 Act. sub. pre. λύνω, aor. λύσω. Fut. θὰ λύνω, θὰ λύσω. Cond. θὰ ἔλυνα.

5 Act. ind. per. ἔχω λύσει, ἔχω λυμένο. Ptc. λύνοντας indeclinable.

6 Pas. ind. pre.	λύν-ομαι	-εσαι	-εται	-όμαστε	-εστε	-ονται
7 Pas. ind. impf.	ἐλυν-όμουν	-όσουν	-όταν	-όμαστε	-όσαστε	-ονταν

8 Pas. ind. aor. ἐλύθηκα. Imp. pre. λύνου λύνεστε, aor. λύσου λυθῆτε.

9 Pas. sub. pre. λύνομαι, aor. λυθῶ. Fut. θὰ λύνομαι, θὰ λυθῶ. Cond. θὰ ἐλυνόμουν.

10 Pas. ind. per. ἔχω λυθεῖ, εἶμαι λυμένος. Ptc. λυμέν-ος -η -ο.

(2) τιμῶ honour

11 Act. ind. pre.	τιμῶ	τιμᾶς	τιμᾶ	τιμοῦμε	τιμᾶτε	τιμοῦν

12 Act. ind. aor. ἐτίμησα, impf. ἐτιμοῦσα. Imp. pre. τίμα τιμᾶτε, aor. τίμησε, τιμῆστε.

13 Act. sub. pre. τιμῶ, aor. τιμήσω. Fut. θὰ τιμῶ, θὰ τιμήσω. Cond. θὰ ἐτιμοῦσα.

14 Act. ind. per. ἔχω τιμήσει, ἔχω τιμημένο. Ptc. τιμώντας indeclinable.

15 Pas. ind. pre.	τιμ-οῦμαι	-ᾶσαι	-ᾶται	-ούμαστε	-ᾶστε	-οῦνται

16 Pas. ind. aor. ἐτιμήθηκα, impf. ἐτιμούμουν. Imp. pre. τιμοῦ τιμᾶστε, aor. τιμήσου τιμηθῆτε.

17 Pas. sub. pre. τιμοῦμαι, aor. τιμηθῶ. Fut. θὰ τιμοῦμαι, θὰ τιμηθῶ. Cond. θὰ ἐτιμούμουν.

18 Pas. ind. per. ἔχω τιμηθεῖ, εἶμαι τιμημένος. Ptc. τιμημέν-ος -η -ο.

(3) φιλῶ kiss

19 Act. ind. pre.	φιλῶ	φιλεῖς	φιλεῖ	φιλοῦμε	φιλεῖτε	φιλοῦν

20 Act. ind. aor. ἐφίλησα, impf. ἐφιλοῦσα. Imp. pre. φίλει φιλεῖτε, aor. φίλησε φιλῆστε.

21 Act. sub. pre. φιλῶ, aor. φιλήσω. Fut. θὰ φιλῶ, θὰ φιλήσω. Cond. θὰ ἐφιλοῦσα.

22 Act. ind. per. ἔχω φιλήσει, ἔχω φιλημένο. Ptc. φιλώντας indeclinable.

23 Pas. ind. pre.	φιλ-οῦμαι	-εῖσαι	-εῖται	-ούμαστε	-εῖστε	-οῦνται

24 Pas. ind. aor. ἐφιλήθηκα, impf. ἐφιλούμουν.

25 Pas. sub. pre. φιλοῦμαι, aor. φιληθῶ. Fut. θὰ φιλοῦμαι, θὰ φιληθῶ. Cond. θὰ ἐφιλούμουν.

26 Pas. ind. per. ἔχω φιληθεῖ, εἶμαι φιλημένος. Ptc. φιλημέν-ος -η -ο.

F. Paradigms

1	αἰσθάνομαι feel	αἰσθανόμουν		αἰσθάνθηκα	αἴσθημα n. feeling
2	ἀκούω hear	ἄκουα	ἄκουσα	ἀκούστηκα	ἀκοή f. hearing
3	πεθαίνω die	πέθαινα	πέθανα		θάνατος m. death

4	βάλλω βάζω put	ἔβαλα ἔβαζα	ἔβαλα ἔβασα	ἐβάλθηκα	βόλι　　　　n. bullet
5	γίνομαι become	γινόμουν		γίνηκα	γένεση　　　f. birth
6	ἔρχομαι come	ἐρχόμουν	ἦρθα, sub. ἔρθω		ἐρχομός　　m. arrival
7	βρίσκω find	ἔβρισκα	ηὖρα, sub. βρῶ	βρέθηκα	βρέσιμο　　n. a find
8	ἔχω have	εἶχα			
9	θαυμάζω wonder	ἐθαύμαζα	ἐθαύμασα		θάμα　　　　n. a wonder
10	μένω stay	ἔμενα	ἔμεινα		μόνος alone
11	παθαίνω suffer	ἐπάθαινα	ἔπαθα		πάθος　　　n. suffering
12	πείθω persuade	ἔπειθα	ἔπεισα	ἐπείστηκα	πιθανός probable
13	πήζω curdle	ἔπηζα	ἔπηξα	ἐπήχτηκα	πηχτή　　　f. jelly
14	σώνω save	ἔσωνα	ἔσωσα	ἐσώθηκα	σωστός correct
15	θρέφω nourish	ἔθρεφα	ἔθρεψα	ἐτράφηκα ἐθρέφτηκα	θροφή　　　f. nourishment
16	τυχαίνω happen	ἐτύχαινα	ἔτυχα		τύχη　　　　f. luck
17	φαίνομαι appear	ἐφαινόμουν		ἐφάνηκα	φανερός clear
18	φέρνω carry, bring	ἔφερνα	ἔφερα	ἐφέρθηκα	φέρσιμο　　n. behaviour
19	φροντίζω care	ἐφρόντιζα	ἐφρόντισα		φροντίδα　f. care

Notes.

A. 1. In addition to the above, the following types of substantive should
be noted: (1) παπᾶς m. 'priest' (acc. gen. παπᾶ, pl. NA παπάδες, G
παπάδων), cf. AG φαγᾶς, ὑαλᾶς etc.; (2) ἀλεποῦ f. 'fox' (A ἀλεποῦ,
G ἀλεποῦς, pl. NA ἀλεποῦδες, G ἀλεπούδων).

TABLE XVI   THE MG NOUN AND VERB   99

B. 2. The adverbs are formed in -α (n. pl.): σοφά σοφώτερα, βαριά βαρύτερα.

C. 3. Like ἕνας μία ἕνα: καθένας (καθείς) καθεμία καθένα 'everyone', κανένας (κανείς) καμμία κανένα 'anyone', gen. sg. m. καθένος, κανενός (see XIV.3.21). From καθένας is formed κάθε indecl. 'every'.

D. 4. The relative ποὺ is used as follows: (1) ὁ ἄνθρωπος ποὺ ἦρθε 'the man who came'; (2) ὁ ἄνθρωπος ποὺ τὸν εἶδα 'the man that I saw'.

   5. The emphatic forms of the possesive pronoun are ὁ δικός μου etc. (δικός < εἰδικός).

E. 6. The augment is not normally carried on verbs beginning with a vowel (ἀκούω ἄκουσα) and may be omitted in other verbs when it is unaccented (λύθηκα for ἐλύθηκα).

   7. The imperative third person is supplied by ἂς (AG ἄφες, imp. aor.ᵃ sg. 2 of ἀφίημι), negative ἂς μή, with the subjunctive: ἂς ἔρθουν 'let them come'.

   8. For τιμῶ etc. we also find τιμ-άεις -άει -ᾶμε -ᾶτε, also for ἐτιμοῦσα etc. ἐτίμα-γα -γες -γε.

   9. The ending -μουν also appears in the form -μουνα (ἐλυνόμουνα), and the endings -ουν -αν -σουν -ταν in the forms -ουνε -ανε -σουνε -τανε (λύνουνε, ἐλύνανε, ἐλυθήκανε, ἐλυνόσουνε, ἐλυνότανε).

   10. For the pas. ind. pre. φιλοῦμαι etc. we also find φιλιέμαι φιλιέσαι φιλιέται φιλιούμαστε φιλιέστε φιλιοῦνται.

   11. Many verbs of the type φιλῶ may also be inflected according to the type τιμῶ, e.g. λυποῦμαι or λυπᾶμαι, θυμοῦμαι or θυμᾶμαι. Many verbs in -ίζω -ύνω -ύω have been attracted to this type, the aorists being homophonous: ξυπνῶ ξύπνησα for ξυπνίζω ξύπνισα, cf. βαρῶ < βαρύνω, μηνῶ < μηνύω.

   12. The negative particles are δέν (AG οὐδέν) and μή(ν), which correspond to AG οὐ and μή, except that δέν, not μή, is used with ἄν 'if'.

   13. In derivatives of AG verbs compounded with prepositions, the preposition is merged with the verb stem: μπαίνω (AG ἐμβαίνω), βγάλω (AG ἐκβάλλω), πεθαίνω πέθανα (AG ἀπέθανον), ξεπέφτω ξέπεσα (AG ἐξέπεσον).

BIBLIOGRAPHY

Chapter I

Vendryes, J., Le langage (Paris, 1921), ch. I-III.

Chapters II-III

Cassirer, E., Philosophie der symbolischen Formen (Berlin, 1923-29), vol. I.
Emerson, O. F., History of the English Language. New York, 1894.
Hudson-Williams, T., A Short Introduction to the Study of Comparative Grammar (Indo-European). Cardiff, 1935.
Meillet, A., Introduction a l'étude comparative des langues indo-européennes. 8 ed. Paris, 1937.
——, Linguistique générale et linguistique historique. Paris, 1921.
Pavlov, P., Selected Works. Moscow, 1955.
Sapir, E., Language: an Introduction to the Study of Speech. New York, 1921.
——, Selected Writings on Language, Culture and Personality. Berkeley, 1949.
Sommerfelt, A., La langue et la société. Oslo, 1938.
Thomson, G., Studies in Ancient Greek Society, Vol. II (London, 1955), ch. 1.
Wells, H. K., Pavlov and Freud (London, 1956), vol. I.

Chapter IV

Diringer, D., The Alphabet. London, 1947.
Karlgren, B., Sound and Symbol in Chinese. London, 1923.
Moorhouse, A. C., Writing and the Alphabet. London, 1946.

Chapters V-IX

Buck, C. D., Comparative Grammar of Greek and Latin. Chicago, 1933.
Chantraine, P., Grammaire homérique. Paris, 1942.
——, Morphologie historique du grec. Paris, 1945.
Lejeune, M., Traité de phonétique grecque. 2 ed. Paris, 1955.
Meillet, A. and Vendryes, J., Traité de grammaire comparée des langues classiques. 2 ed. Paris, 1927.
Stehle, M., Griechische Wortkunde. 7 ed. Stuttgart, 1946.
Thomson, G., The Postponement of Interrogatives in Attic Drama (a study in word-order). Classical Quarterly, vol. XXXIII (1939) p. 147.

Chapter X

Brugmann, K., Die Syntax des einfachen Satzes im Indo-germanischen. Berlin and Leipzig, 1925.
Kieckers, E., Historische griechische Grammatik (Berlin and Leipzig, 1925-26), vols. III-IV.

Chapters XI-XII

Buck, C. D., The Greek Dialects. Chicago, 1955.
Meillet, A., Aperçu d'une histoire de la langue grecque. 4 ed. Paris, 1935.
Thomson, G., Studies in Ancient Greek Society, Vol. I (2 ed. London, 1954), ch. XVI.

Chapters XIII-XIV

Andriotis, N. P., 'Ετυμολογικὸ λέξικο τῆς κοινῆς νεοελληνικῆς, Athens, 1951.
Bachtin, N., Introduction to the Study of Modern Greek. Cambridge, 1935.
Cantarella, R., I poeti bizantini. 2 vols. Milan, 1948.
Hesseling, D. C. and Pernot, H., Chrestomathie néo-hellenique. Paris, 1925.
Pernot, H., Chansons populaires grecs. Paris, 1931.
Politis, N., 'Εκλογαὶ ἀπὸ τὰ τραγούδια τοῦ 'Ελληνικοῦ λαοῦ. 3 ed. Athens, 1932.
Thumb, A., Die griechische Sprache im Zeitalter des Hellenismus. Strassburg, 1901.
——, Handbook of the Modern Greek Vernacular. Edinburgh, 1912.
Triantaphyllidis, M. A., Νεοελληνικὴ γραμματική: 'Ιστορικὴ εἰσαγωγή. Athens, 1938.
Valetas, G., 'Ανθολογία τῆς δημοτικῆς πεζογραφίας. 3 vols. Athens, 1947-49.

By the same author

Greek Lyric Metre. Cambridge, 1929. Second edition, 1960.
Breith Báis ar Eagnaidhe. The Apology, Crito and Phaedo, translated into Irish. Dublin, 1929.
Aeschylus, Prometheus Bound, edited with introduction, commentary and translation. Cambridge, 1932.
Euripidés, Alcéstis, edited with introduction and commentary (in Irish). Dublin, 1932.
Fiche Blian ag Fás, by Maurice O'Sullivan, edited by G. T. Dublin, 1933. Twenty Years A-Growing, translated from the Irish. London, 1933. New York, 1933. Translated into French, German and Czech. 'World's Classics' edition (revised) Oxford, 1953.
Aeschylus, Prométheus fé chuibhreach, edited with introduction and commentary (in Irish). Dublin, 1933.
Tosnú na Feallsúnachta. A short history of early Greek philosophy (in Irish). Dublin, 1935.
Leabhar na n-Urnaihí Cóchoiteanna. The Book of Common Prayer, translated into Irish for the Church of Ireland by G. T. in collaboration with the late Prof. O. Bergin. Dublin, 1938.
Aeschylus, Oresteia, edited with introduction, translation, and a commentary in which is included the work of the late Walter G. Headlam. 2 vols. Cambridge, 1938.
Aeschylus and Athens: a study in the social origins of drama. London, 1941. Second edition, 1945. Translated into Italian, German, Czech, Polish, Hungarian, Greek, and Hebrew.
Marxism and Poetry. London, 1946. New York, 1946. Second edition: Bombay, 1953. Third edition: New Delhi, 1954. Translated into French, Slovak, Hungarian, Greek, Arabic, Chinese (two editions), and Japanese.
Studies in Ancient Greek Society. Vol. I: The Prehistoric Aegean. London, 1949. Second edition, 1954. Translated into Czech, German, Polish, Russian, Greek and Japanese.
Studies in Ancient Greek Society. Vol. II: The First Philosophers. London, 1955. Second edition, 1961. Translated into Czech, Spanish, Russian, Chinese and Japanese.
Διαλέξεις γιὰ τὸν ἀρχαῖο ἑλληνικὸ πολιτισμό. 2 vols. Athens, 1962.
'Η ἑλληνικὴ γλώσσα ἀρχαία καὶ νέα. Athens, 1964.
Aeschylus, the Oresteia and the Prometheus Bound, translated into English verse, with an introduction. New York, 1965.

A new edition of the Headlam-Thomson Oresteia is in the press.